AXIS BLOCKADE RUNNERS
OF WORLD WAR II

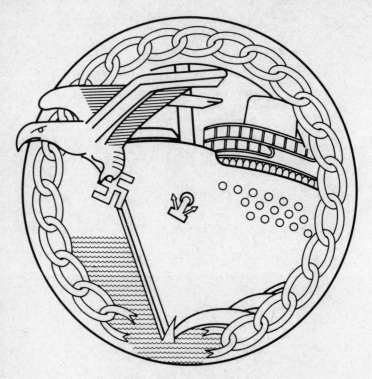

The blockade runners' badge.

AXIS BLOCKADE RUNNERS
OF WORLD WAR II

Martin Brice

Naval Institute Press

© Martin Brice 1981
First published 1981

Published and distributed in the United States of
America and Canada by the Naval Institute Press,
Annapolis, Maryland 21402

Library of Congress Catalog Card No. 81-80883

ISBN 0-87021-908-1

Printed in Great Britain

Contents

List of Illustrations

24. The US cruiser *Omaha* closing the German blockade runner *Odenwald* in the South Atlantic on 6 November 1941.

25. Short of fuel, the destroyer *Somers* rigged a sail to assist fuel economy while escorting *Odenwald* to Trinidad.

26. *Elsa Essberger* seen here in ballast prewar.

27. The British cruiser *Dunedin* in Freetown, 1940.

28. A photograph of *Cortellazzo* taken when Italy was still neutral.

29. The US cruiser *Savannah* intercepted *Karin* on 10 March 1943.

30. *Pietro Orseolo*, who did a round trip from Japan to Bordeaux and back again.

31. Hamburg–Amerika's *Osorno* was the only surface blockade runner to reach France in the winter of 1943–4.

32. A US Navy Consolidated PB4Y Liberator crosses the Cornish coast on a Biscay patrol.

33. The last blockade runner; *U532* at Liverpool in May 1945.

Acknowledgment

For help, information, advice and encouragement I am grateful to the following individuals and organizations.

Aldershot Library; D.C. Allard, Head of the Operational Archives Branch of the US Navy Historical Center; Alton Library; A.T. Boden; Sir Frank Bowden; British Library; F. Brookshaw; Deutsche Afrika–Linien GmbH & John T. Essberger; Frank E. Dodman; George J. Duke; George E. Finch; Gordon Frater; Heinz Kurt Gast; Hamburg-Südamerikanische DG; Hansa DDG; Hapag–Lloyd AG; Imperial War Museum, Departments of Photographs and Printed Books; Lieutenant-Commander H.M. Irwin; S. Jacobs; P.M. Jervis; G.G. Kaye; W. H. Longstaff; Loughton Library; James S. Lucas; Kenneth J. Ludwig; Don McKeggie; National Maritime Museum; Ministry of Defence, Naval Library; The Editor, *Navy News;* Reinhard Nehrlich; Poplar Central Library, Merchant Navy Collection; Portsmouth Central Library, Naval Collection; Harold C. Potterton; Public Record Office, Kew; Red House Museum, Christchurch; Prof. Dr. Jürgen Rohwer & the Bibliothek für Zeitgeschichte, Stuttgart; Royal United Services Institute; The Editor, *Sea Breezes;* Donald H. Shore; Lieutenant-Commander Charles McD. Stuart; Ludolf Timm; Commander Seymour Tuke; Edward A. Wilson; and Winchester Central Reference and Lending Libraries.

Those who provided illustrations were as follows:
F. Brookshaw: 2.
Deutsche Afrika-Linien GmbH & John T. Essberger: 9; 26.
George E. Finch: 6.
Hapag-Lloyd AG: 4; 15.
Imperial War Museum: 3; 7; 18; 22; 32; 33.
S. Jacobs: 1; 14.
National Maritime Museum: 5; 10; 11; 12; 13; 21; 27; 29.
Reinhard Nehrlich: 8.
Ludolf Timm: 23.
United States Naval Historical Center: 24; 25.
Edward A. Wilson: 17; 19; 20; 28; 30; 31.
My thanks are also due to the unknown leading telegraphist of HMS *Maloja's* ship's company, who took the photograph which was loaned by Mr D.H. Shore: 16.

Transcripts of Crown Copyright records in the Public Record Office appear by permission of the Controller of Her Majesty's Stationery Office.

In addition I must acknowledge the Oxford University Press for the verse on page 153. It was written by Arthur Hugh Clough (1819–61), and has been quoted from *The Oxford Book of Victorian Verse*, edited by Arthur Quiller-Couch and published by Clarendon Press in 1912, being republished in 1948.

Author's Note

Tonnage

That of merchant ships is usually quoted in gross tons, warship size as displacement. The amount of consignments is given in tons weight, but original sources do not always indicate whether they are referring to tons avoirdupois or tonnes metric. Any discrepancy is slight and so the word 'ton' has been used throughout the book.

Metric Conversions

These have only been given where they seem appropriate, as a comparison of armaments, for example. In such instances, the calibre is first given in the normal measurement of the operating navy, and then converted to imperial or metric as necessary. German calibres were usually expressed in centimetres, French and Italian in millimetres.

Times

In its simplest form, one action may have four sets of times by which the sequence of events was recorded: local British time, local German time, British Admiralty time and Kriegsmarine Berlin time. The Admiralty time may be Greenwich Mean Time, British Summer Time, or Double Summer Time. What seems to be the local British ship time, may in fact be such, or it may be that recorded by the local C-in-C, whose area may be so big that his headquarters is in a different time zone. The participation of American forces can add similar permutations. Obviously there were wartime procedures for identifying which time was being used, but later sources, even official ones, can give quite different times according to nationality. And when these events occurred around midnight, this can result in a different date. In this book I have endeavoured to use the 12-hour clock with 'am' and 'pm' for local time, so that people have their meals at the proper time of day. I have used the 24-hour clock without '-hrs,' as official time, which may or may not be the same as local ship time.

1 The Blockade Runners

Out of the east they came, their wake the golden rays of the rising sun. Astern, hidden behind that glowing disc, lay the islands and continents, the smells and noises, the colours and peoples, the uncertain navigation and inquisitive spies of the Orient. Ahead lay the concealing vastness of the Indian Ocean and the eternal swell of the great Antarctic drift.

Out of the south they came, their wake snow-white and bar-straight to the cloudless, still horizon. Far astern now were the wandering albatross and the floating ice. Now flying fish and dolphins paced the bow and for a moment became creatures of the air.

Out of the west they came, their wake unseen among Atlantic seas, each pursuing wave lifting the stern, giving thousands of tons of man-made vessel a perceptible shove along its way. Astern were the fogs of the Newfoundland Banks. Ahead lay the ports of Europe, and the patrols of the enemy.

Out of the north they came with hardly any wake at all, slipping down glassy fjord and lead, dark against the darker mountains. Astern lay lonely, spartan harbours and the aurora borealis. Ahead were the havens of home, the pinnacles of uncharted rocks, the traps and ambushes of the enemy.

Out of the east and the south, out of the west and the north came the blockade runners, bearing tin for the alloys used in white metal bearings and wolfram for tungsten-carbide and for those hardened steels without which no machine tools could be made. They carried capacious tanks full of edible oils, constituents of margarine and other foodstuffs to sustain the fighting man, strengthen the sinews of the munitions worker, and nourish the citizens of the future. The blockade runners shipped wood pulp and coffee, gemstones and drugs. Some carried passengers—just a few—but each man with a skill vital to the war effort, a knowledge of radio or radar, a machine-like ability to crack the most difficult code, a chemist, an experienced seaman, an enthusiastic recruit, a diplomat with inside information. Most important of all, the blockade runners carried rubber, raw natural rubber that flexed and bounced, and was the only really good material for the tyres of army trucks juddering across steppes and deserts and for the tyres of bombers, fighters, transports and trainers thudding onto airfields from Norway to Libya and from Brittany to the Caucasus.

Out of the east and the south, the west and the north came *Bremen*, *Konsul Horn*, *Wangoni*, *Himalaya*, *Anneliese Essberger*, *Portland*, *Fusijama* and *Rio Grande* —*Rio Grande*, a German ship with a Latin–American name who escaped interception more times than any other Axis blockade runner, although the Italian *Pietro Orseolo* closely paralleled her success.

Rio Grande was almost brand-new at the beginning of World War II, having been launched by Howaldtswerke of Hamburg on 17 January 1939. Completed on 27 March 1939, she measured 6062 gross tons, with a carrying capacity of 9425 deadweight tons. *Rio Grande* was 476¾ feet long and 61½ feet wide, with a draught of 24 feet (in metres, 145.3 x 18.7 x 7.3). Her eight-cylinder diesel engine had been constructed by Maschinenfabrik, Augsburg–Nürnberg of Augsburg. It delivered 3350 hp (registering 909 nominal hp) which gave the freighter a speed of 13 knots. Her owners were the Hamburg–Südamerikanische Dampfschiffahrtsgesellschaft of Hamburg and she had been operating on the South American service when war began in September 1939.

For over a year *Rio Grande* and her crew of thirty-five waited in her namesake port of Rio Grande do Sul, sheltered by Brazilian neutrality from the Royal Navy outside. It was not until late 1940 that it was time for her to make a move. Her master (Kapitän J. Heins), First Officer Heinrich von Allwörden and Second Officer Hans Georg Erhardt, had made sure that *Rio Grande* would be ready whenever the order came. Besides keeping the ship in good condition, they had conserved the fuel in her bunkers which were much larger than British agents thought. The crew's health and interest had been maintained by sporting activities, which had also facilitated contacts with sources of information about Royal Navy movements. Sailing instructions were received from the German consulate, but delay was caused by the arrival of three British cargo ships. They could easily have shadowed the German, and it was not until the last had left the port that Kapitän Heins judged that it was safe to sail.

With two tugs in charge, *Rio Grande* was free of her familiar berth at 6.03 on the evening of Thursday, 31 October 1940. Her crew knew that enemy spies would observe and report this, but ships often shift from quay to anchorage to wharf to dock for a variety of reasons. In the gathering darkness it would be some time before it was realized that this was no routine harbour movement, but departure.

The tugs eased *Rio Grande* through the shallow-draught lake boats linking the port with the German pioneering settlements around Porto Allegre. The lights of the twin cities of Rio Grande do Sul and Sao José do Norte dropped astern, replaced by eight miles of low blackness on either side of the wide Great

River, debouching the waters of landlocked Lagoa dos Patos. Then, in the dredged channel cut through the 26-foot submerged bar at the river mouth, *Rio Grande* took the mud. For two and a half hours she was held there, until the tugs pulled her clear. The tow was slipped at 10.07 pm and the pilot dropped an hour later. *Rio Grande* was on her way with 6948 tons of cargo for Germany's war effort.

A British agent logged her time of departure as 10.10 pm. He told Intelligence that she was heading north, but that later she had completely reversed course. Next day a Royal Navy signal was describing *Rio Grande* and instructing British warships to look out for her. The nearest were the cruiser *Enterprise* and the armed merchant cruisers (AMCs) *Queen of Bermuda* and *Asturias*, 1200 and 286 miles away respectively. The time of origin (TOO) of *Asturias'* instructions was 0847, but because reception from the Falkland Islands' transmitter was very bad, the complete message was not taken in until 1900. By then a gap had been left to the south of Rio Grande do Sul, while the search was further diverted by encountering an Argentinian ship also called *Rio Grande*.

For nine days the German *Rio Grande* was alone. Once clear of the coast Kapitän Heins headed approximately east by north to a secret South Atlantic rendezvous between Trinidad and Tristan da Cunha. Codenamed *Andalusien*, it was one of those relatively calm mid-ocean areas that were not too far from regular shipping lanes, yet were rarely traversed by any vessel. It was here that *Rio Grande* met the disguised raider *Thor*, now beginning her sixth month at sea. The freighter's hatches were opened up, useful items in the cargo being hoisted out and transferred to *Thor*. The latter took this opportunity to get rid of 315 prisoners from the eight merchant ships so far sunk or captured. They and their guards were accommodated in *Rio Grande*, who had been disguised as her near-sister *Belgrano*, just to confuse any prisoners who might escape to tell what they had seen. *Rio Grande* then concluded her brief role as raider supply ship and the two vessels parted company.

During the northward voyage, there were the usual problems of food, drink and exercise for a large number of prisoners, who put about rumours of an escape to unmask an informer. Several merchant ships were sighted, one tanker being passed at night at a distance of 500 yards, but nothing happened. Recently British submarines had intercepted returning prizes in the Bay of Biscay, but whatever hopes or fears *Rio Grande*'s passengers and crew may have had were not realized. Armed with a wooden gun, the freighter passed on time through the various points ordered by Seekriegsleitung (the German Navy's Operations Division, known as SKL) and reached Bordeaux on 14 December 1940.

Until 1941, the blockade runners' aim was safe arrival in Axis harbours with cargoes loaded at their usual peacetime ports. From this year onwards, the German authorities began a direct service between Japan and Europe. Suitable ships had to be fast, efficient, large enough to carry a worthwhile quantity of cargo, and be capable of voyaging over halfway round the world without refuelling. *Rio Grande*, temporarily regarded as a naval tender at Bordeaux, met all these requirements. Refitted, armed with a 15-cm (5.9-inch) gun, and commanded by Kapitän von Allwörden, she slipped down the Gironde on 21 September 1941 with a general cargo, mainly manufactured goods. Such eastbound consignments frequently included amounts of piano wire, ideal for the construction of springs. When away from the danger area, *Rio Grande* left behind her covering U-boats. Down through the South Atlantic she went, rounding Cape Horn and heading northwestwards across the broad Pacific. She passed between Hawaii and Phoenix Island and docked at Osaka on 6 December 1941.

Next day Japan was at war. It hardly affected *Rio Grande*'s schedule. She completed loading across the bay at Kobe and sailed from there on the last day of January 1942. This time she was routed through the islands of the South Pacific, far from the sensitive area near Pearl Harbor and the desperate battles in the Philippines and South-East Asia. Already much of this area was controlled by the Japanese, although that proved of no comfort to Kapitän von Allwörden. 'An unidentified merchantman here must be a hostile transport,' logically reasoned the Japanese pilot who brought his aircraft roaring over *Rio Grande*. Fortunately his bombs all missed, although one splinter ricocheted onto the deck. The freighter went on, deep into the Antarctic, way beyond Cape Horn, before turning north again to berth in Bordeaux on 10 April 1942.

As the harbour tug eased *Rio Grande* in stern-first, her crew could see the parade drawn up on the quayside. Konteradmiral (Rear-Admiral) Menche, (the head of the Kriegsmarinedienstelle or Navy Service Office in Bordeaux, known as KMD) had come to welcome them in person. There were bands, flowers, and a special visit to Grossadmiral (Grand-Admiral) Raeder in Berlin. Kapitän von Allwörden could not see what all the fuss was about. Merchant seamen were quite used to arriving in harbour after a 34,000-mile round trip with ship, cargo and crew intact. That was what their job was all about.

Another refit was called for. Extra fuel and water tanks and another gun were installed by the time *Rio Grande* next sailed on 28 September 1942, again exporting equipment, machinery and other items as vital to the Japanese war effort as rubber was to Germany. Almost at once she was attacked by two Short Sunderland flying boats and had to seek temporary shelter in the neutral Spanish port of El Ferrol. Kapitän von Allwörden was then routed west of the Azores, clear of the dangerous focal area between Cape Finisterre and the approaches to Gibraltar. Near the fogs of the Newfoundland Grand Banks, he steered southwards, but his worries were not yet over, not even when he had passed through the narrowest part of the South Atlantic. Midway and Guadalcanal had made the central and South Pacific too hot for Axis surface ships, while South-East Asia was now in Japanese hands. So *Rio Grande*, like all blockade runners from the middle of 1942 onwards, took the 11,000-mile Good Hope route. She left the Cape well to port and entered the Indian Ocean, making for the Sunda Strait between Java and Sumatra. At some time she would have to traverse the British convoy routes from Australia. *Ramses*, a Europe-bound blockade runner, had been doing just that when she was spotted by convoy escorts. *Rio Grande* was some distance from this incident, but Kapitän von Allwörden was ordered to mark time while this Allied activity died down—the German authorities could not be certain that this was not a special hunt for blockade runners. Accordingly Kapitän von Allwörden laid off a series of giant zigzags to the west of Australia until it was safe to approach the Japanese defensive perimeter along the East Indies. *Rio Grande*'s course then took her between Borneo and Celebes, and south of the Philippines to arrive in Japan on New Year's Eve 1942.

Turn-around was completed by 28 January 1943. Leaving Yokohama and Tokyo behind, *Rio Grande* proceeded north of the Philippines to call at Singapore before passing through the Sunda Strait. But Allied maritime strength was growing. There were warships all over the Indian Ocean covering troop convoys. In the Atlantic, reinforced cruiser patrols had intercepted nearly all the recent blockade runners, both east- and westbound. Coastal Command was making it almost impossible for any German vessel to cross the Bay of Biscay. The days would be even longer by the time *Rio Grande* appeared in the area. So Kapitän von Allwörden was instructed to turn his ship around. For a while, north of the Philippines, the crew wondered if there had been another change of plan, but after another brief period of aimless zigzagging, they were soon back in Japan.

The employment of operational U-boats as blockade runners during 1943 enabled Germany and Japan to exchange token amounts of cargo pending the construction of proper transport submarines. German industry could not wait for that programme to come to fruition. By the winter of 1943, several full cargoes were needed at once, and not in a couple of years' time. Surface merchant vessels must try to get through. It would be a desperate gamble, but it must be tried.

Perhaps if the five motor vessels already in Japan made the attempt fairly close together, they would baffle the Allied patrols, the interception of one diverting attention from another. In mid-ocean they would have to rely on their own initiative and armament, but something could be done to help them in the most dangerous area approaching Europe. Escort forces were strengthened in French ports and the importance of covering these operations stressed upon U-boat commanders.

Besides their usual cargoes of rubber and other products (totalling 33,095 tons) the blockade runners would be carrying five men under arrest for various crimes. Because one was said to have been a Communist member of Richard

Sorge's Lucy spy ring in Japan, the head of the Gestapo in Tokyo had insisted that all five (including those guilty of lesser felonies) should suffer the severest punishment. All must be left in their cells if the ships had to be scuttled, lest further treason be committed when they were rescued by the Allies. Admiral Wenneker, the Naval Attaché in Tokyo, was not happy about this order and asked for confirmation from SKL in Berlin. As this had not arrived before the blockade runners were due to sail, he handed the written order to the captains concerned, trying to convey in conversation that it might not be binding.

The ships sailed at such intervals that escorting destroyers could rendezvous with each individual runner 400 miles out, take her into Bordeaux, and sail again to meet the next. The most favourable time would be the middle of the winter of 1943-4, the significance of this period being equally apparent to Britain's Ministry of Economic Warfare. Photographic reconnaissance betrayed the reinforcement of the Biscay warships, while further information was obtained from the interpretation of wireless traffic and from agents' reports in the Far East.

The interception of these five blockade runners became a major operation in itself. American, British, French, Italian, Brazilian and New Zealand cruisers, destroyers, escort carriers, corvettes, Liberators, Wildcats, Halifaxes, Sunderlands, Mosquitoes, Beaufighters, Stirlings, Mariners and Kingfishers were deployed from the Cape of Good Hope to the English Channel. It would need a lot of luck to get past all those watching eyes.

So far the five merchant ships and their crews had had a lot of luck. They were also experienced. Kapitän Paul Hellmann's *Osorno*, owned by Hamburg-Amerikanisches Pakete Aktien Gesellschaft (HAPAG) had already done one round trip to and from Europe. *Alsterufer*, at 2729 tons the smallest of the team, was a refrigerated ship belonging to Robert M. Sloman Jr of Hamburg. She had been built by Eriksberg at Gothenburg in Sweden just before the war began. She had served as a supply ship for surface raiders before coming out to Japan from Bordeaux. Her master was Kapitän Piatek, while Kapitän Krage was in command of *Weserland*. She was the oldest of the little fleet, having been built by Blohm und Voss in 1922 for HAPAG. She had then been called *Ermland*, and it was under that name that she had made the very first through passage from the Far East to the Gironde back in December 1940—April 1941. She was renamed *Weserland* in 1942 to avoid confusion with another *Ermland* then serving as a Kriegsmarine (naval) auxiliary. After returning to Japan, she had made another attempt to reach Europe earlier in 1943, but had been recalled. The largest, HAPAG's *Burgenland*, grossing 7320 tons, had a similar record and was commanded by Kapitän Schutz. And then there was *Rio Grande*.

She was the third in the order of sailing, from Yokohama on 4 October 1943. *Weserland* and *Burgenland* did not get under way until later in the month, but already Allied agents in Saigon were reporting that the first three had called there. All unknowing, the ships went on their way. Once more Kapitän von Allwörden took *Rio Grande* through the Sunda Strait. Once more Krakatoa, scene of the biggest bang in recorded history, was left astern. Once more the freighter's bows cleft the Indian Ocean and plunged into the southern swell. Then, as had happened before, came fresh instructions to mark time, zigzag slowly across the South Atlantic, so as to be just two days ahead of *Weserland* and *Burgenland*.

Far out in front, Kapitän Hellmann was proving that his *Osorno*'s luck still held. On 8 December 1943, midway between the Brazilian island of Fernando Noronha and Ascension, a four-engined landplane with twin fin and rudder found them—a Consolidated PB4Y Liberator. It had come from the United States Navy Bomber Squadron (Bombron) 107 on Ascension. Its pilot was suspicious, but he did not want to bomb what might prove to be a friendly but signally inefficient merchantman. Nor, if truly a blockade runner, did he wish to destroy a cargo of rubber of great value to the Allies. A warship would be able to board the stranger. So for forty minutes the aircraft observed *Osorno* and then made off. The pilot intended to guide in the American cruiser *Marblehead* and her accompanying destroyer, but these two units were already investigating another sighting, which was in fact a friendly independent. It was three hours before their attention could be turned to the PB4Y's report. Almost at once they were involved in a hunt for *U510*, one of the big Type IXD2 submarines on passage to the Indian Ocean to act as a returning undersea blockade runner. But *U510* escaped—and so did *Osorno*.

Her luck held as she turned eastwards off the Newfoundland Banks without being sighted again. It held on 18 December when she satisfied a Sunderland that she was the British ship *Landsman* on independent passage from Cape Town to Liverpool. That night the shape of a destroyer was glimpsed through the darkness. She was obviously British and it was also obvious that she had seen *Osorno*. Now close enough to use his loudhailer, the English commander warned *Osorno* to watch out for U-boats and ordered her to keep clear. Kapitän Hellmann replied that he could not make the required course and would have to stop. What would the next instruction be? It never came. The British warship swung away and began depth-charging a suspicious asdic contact. The two vessels lost sight of each other, and *Osorno*'s identity was still her own secret.

So too was her exact position, even to the German authorities. The Luftwaffe was ordered to look for her and on 20 December thirteen U-boats were formed into Gruppe *Borkum* to cover *Osorno*'s possible route. The resulting radio signals were picked up and an American support group consisting of the escort carrier *Card* and the destroyers *Leary*, *Schenk* and *Decatur* was ordered to locate this force of U-boats. However, it was *Card* who was sighted first, by German long-range aircraft. Their reports caused Grossadmiral Dönitz to deploy the U-boats of Gruppe *Borkum* against Captain Isbell's American warships, thus distracting them from *Osorno*. The very next day (23 December) a single-seat Grumman FM-1 Wildcat fighter which had been catapulted from *Card*'s heaving flight-deck, reported a merchantman heading southeast. She could not give the correct answer when challenged, even though wearing the Red Ensign.

But *Osorno*'s luck still held. No destroyers appeared over the tossing horizon— they were too low on fuel for any high-speed diversion and they were suffering from the bad weather. Nor could they be detached from the carrier's screen when U-boats were known to be in the vicinity. No more aircraft dived on *Osorno;* the stormy seas caused accidents on *Card*'s flight-deck and prevented further flying operations. And that night, their movements reported by Luft-waffe planes taking off from solid runways in France, *Card* and her old flush-deck destroyers were fully occupied fighting off the *Borkum* U-boats. The escort carrier escaped three zigzagging torpedoes and *Decatur* evaded an acoustic torpedo. *Schenk* ran down the source of another acoustic torpedo to depth-charge and sink *U645*, but yet another of such weapons was launched by her sister-boat *U275*. It homed in and exploded on *Leary*'s propellers, further—and fatal—damage being inflicted by *U382*. The incidents of this night were repeated twenty-four hours later, when Gruppe *Borkum* encountered a British convoy, the destroyer *Hurricane* being sunk by an acoustic torpedo from *U305*.

Through this storm-tossed battlefield steered *Osorno*. Her luck still held, but at daylight on Christmas Morning she was being shadowed by Sunderlands from Nos. 201 (RAF), 422 (RCAF) and 461 (RAAF) Squadrons. One came too close. *Osorno* opened fire and drove it off; as far as they could tell it crashed in the sea. Then at a cloudy midday, about 450 miles out from the Gironde, *Osorno*'s lookouts saw the low shapes of destroyers—destroyers and torpedo boats with familiar funnel caps. It was Kapitän zür See (Captain) Erdmenger with the 8th Zerstörer (Destroyer) Flotille and the 4th Torpedoboote Flotille. 'Frohe Weinachten' ('Merry Christmas') signalled Kapitän Hellmann.

Within an hour the eleven Narviks and Elbings had ranged themselves around *Osorno*, a comforting total of 207 guns from 2-cm (.8-inch) to 15-cm (5.9-inch), plus seventy-six torpedoes in case the English cruisers from Plymouth and the Azores came too close. Overhead were Junkers Ju88 fighters. Even so the RAF Handley Page Halifaxes came in, eight of them from No. 502 Squad-ron. From 1620 to 1915 they struck at the German force, Q *for Queen* claiming a hit on one of the ships. It was certainly not *Osorno;* her luck still held.

It still held through succeeding attacks as darkness closed in and prevented fifty-eight de Havilland Mosquitoes and torpedo-carrying Bristol Beaufighters from finding her. It was still holding out as she entered the security of the 200-yard wide swept channel of the Gironde in the earliest glimmer of dawn on 26 December. Minensuchboote (M-boote or minesweepers) took over the escort while the destroyers fuelled. *Osorno* had come halfway round the world— and then her luck ran out.

Back on 14 June 1943, the mine-clearance vessel *Sperrbrecher 21* (formerly the merchant ship *Nestor*) had detonated a mine and foundered off Royan. Her wreck still partially fouled the fog-bound channel and onto it ran *Osorno*. Some of her luck still hovered about her, for she stayed afloat long enough to be beached at Le Verdon. Salvage experts considered that most of her cargo could be saved, which was done in spite of a subsequent minelaying operation by Short Stirlings of the RAF. For his efforts in getting his ship in, Kapitän Hellmann was awarded the Knight's Cross of the Iron Cross, the only civilian to be so honoured.

Past *Osorno* slipped the destroyers and torpedo boats making for the open sea to meet *Alsterufer*, the next blockade runner on the list. She had been even more fortunate than *Osorno* in the South Atlantic narrows, having passed through without being sighted at all. *Alsterufer* spent Christmas Day alone in the North Atlantic, all festivities and bottle-openings being postponed until arrival in Bordeaux could occasion a double celebration. She remained undetected until 10.15 am on 27 December, when about 500 miles northwest of Cape Finisterre. Her gunners made the intercepting Sunderland (*T for Tare* from No. 201 Squadron) keep its distance. For two and half hours it circled, broadcasting its position and being joined by Sunderlands *Q for Queen* of No. 422 (RCAF) Squadron and another No. 201 Squadron machine (*U for Uncle*). Then *T/Tare* turned and came roaring in to be greeted again by *Alsterufer*'s gunfire. Its bombs missed. The flying boat climbed away and disappeared towards its home base.

Twice more during the afternoon of cloud and rain, this pattern of attack was repeated without interrupting *Alsterufer*'s 15½-knot dash towards Bordeaux. That secure haven was still a long way off. There was no point in maintaining wireless silence now. Kapitän Piatek broadcast his position. Aircraft and destroyers were on their way, he was told; but the surface vessels would not arrive before morning and no German engine note broke the steady sound of circling Pratt & Whitneys. Some of *Alsterufer*'s off-duty crew, angry at the Luftwaffe's failure to protect them, stayed on deck staring at the hostile sky. Others went below to the mess aft, trying to forget their worries by concentrating on a game of chess.

Then it was the turn of a Liberator, *H for How*, flown by Pilot Officer O. Dolezal of No. 311 (Czech) Squadron, to reach his point of longest endurance. He made his approach from the south, on *Alsterufer*'s starboard side. launching his eight underwing rockets. He swept over the target at 600 feet, through the flak, and released two bombs, one of 250 pounds and one of 500 pounds (113-kg and 227-kg). *Alsterufer* was steaming fast, faster than most mercantile targets could be expected to move. The bombs almost missed astern, but not quite; a massive explosion showed Pilot Officer Dolezal ('a cunning old fox' as Kapitän Piatek described him, in Richards & Saunders' *Royal Air Force 1939–1945*), that he had scored a hit right aft. There were signs that five of the rockets had also struck home.

As *H/How* circled for a crew-member to take photographs with a hand-held camera, flames were pouring out of the after hatch. There were more explosions; *Alsterufer*'s bridge and superstructure, the whole after part of the ship, was ablaze. She was going down by the stern; her crew were abandoning ship, taking to liferafts and boats. Even after Pilot Officer Dolezal had turned his Liberator in the direction of Talbenny in Pembrokeshire, two others still circled watching and waiting until the early evening when the glowing hulk went down 750 miles from her destination, leaving fifty-two survivors to be rescued by British corvettes two days later. Other vessels picked up a further twenty-two. The two chess-players were not among them. They had been killed by the Liberator's bomb.

And now it was the New Year of 1944. Now it was *Rio Grande*'s turn. Now she was hurrying up through the South Atlantic, every thud of her diesel, every turn of her screw, taking her nearer those dangerous narrows between West Africa and Brazil. And beyond lay the most hazardous approach through the Bay of Biscay. Now there would be no welcoming destroyers; they had been decimated and scattered during the *Alsterufer* operation. But *Rio Grande*'s luck might still hold out, even if the others' did not. For Kapitän von Allwörden and his men it was a desperate gamble. They knew that. But then, blockade runners had been gambling, sometimes winning, sometimes losing, for centuries.

2 The Rules of the Game

The rival city-states of ancient Greece and their island colonies depended upon seaborne trade for corn, wood, minerals and other raw materials. Such an economy was highly susceptible to blockade and there are many references to the employment of squadrons in this form of warfare. In 425 BC, a force of 420 Spartans plus their personal serfs (or Helots) was trapped on the island of Sphacteria. During the hours of daylight, two Athenian galleys were on continuous patrol, circling the island on opposite courses. At night, seventy warships lay at anchor around Sphacteria, ready to intercept any Spartan attempt to provision their garrison. As the autumn nights became longer and darker, the Athenian watchers, though only 200 yards apart, found it impossible to maintain ceaseless vigil when cables dragged, oars broke or lookouts were half-blinded by flying spray. On such nights, Helots volunteered to man boats, smuggling cargoes of food to their Spartan masters. Successful crews were rewarded with their freedom, plus the necessary gold to set them up in their new life. Even when the seas were calm, a few hardy souls managed to swim silently past the Athenians, towing buoyant skins containing honey mixed with poppy seed and linseed—tasty rations rich in protein and carbohydrates.

This blockade running by a people not noted for maritime prowess was, strictly speaking, a military operation rather than the maintenance of a civil community. Nevertheless, the Helots hazarded themselves voluntarily, not because they were under martial obligation. The fact that they expected no personal gain afterwards does not detract from the risks they ran. That they were prepared to help their Spartan masters at all, demonstrates their patriotism; reward was an extra bonus.

The methods they employed must have been typical of many, often ill-fated attempts to relieve the hunger—and greed—of blockaded noncombatants in ancient times. Certainly the reliance on a combination of bad weather, stealth and audacity, instead of fighting a way through, is a theme repeated in every blockade runner's career. Another is the diversion caused by the interception of one blockade runner, enabling another to escape. This happened during the 1745 Rebellion, when two ships which had set out with the Young Pretender were found off the Lizard by *HMS Lion*. While the privateer *Elizabeth* engaged the warship, *Du Teillay* (chartered by the Scots under the name of *Doutelle*) made off bearing Prince Charles Edward Stewart and his 'Seven Men of Moidart' safely on their way. Unfortunately, the Rebellion's stock of munitions was in the other vessel.

At the beginning of the American Civil War in 1861, President Lincoln announced a blockade of the Confederate Southern States. He did not have enough ships to cover the whole coast, only to watch at certain focal points. According to a confirmatory definition of 1856 warships had to be stationed so closely, or pass along the coast so frequently, that nothing could approach a harbour without being stopped, otherwise it was not a legal blockade. Further, a nation cannot 'blockade' its own coast, it can only 'close' its own ports. Neutrals (mainly Britain) therefore argued that the United States did not have a belligerent's right of search—the very issue which had occasioned the Anglo-American War of 1812. However, diplomatic exchanges resulted in neutral acceptance of the Federals' de facto blockade, by which time the Northern fleet was growing in strength and exerting a stranglehold on Confederate trade.

The Southern Navy tried to break this grip, employing such novel devices as armoured rams and submersible torpedo boats—to no avail. So it was left to lone vessels, either government- or privately-owned, to make their own efforts to slip through. Some had been doing this since the outbreak of hostilities, but later paddlers or screw-steamers were purpose-built. They were of light but sturdy construction, fast (*Will o' the Wisp* reached $17\frac{1}{2}$ knots), and usually unarmed—guns caused legal complications for merchantmen, as well as adding weight. Many were painted off-white for camouflage, for their lack of armament did not mean immunity from hostile gunfire. Only if they stopped and handed their ship over could the crew be certain of saving their lives—and that they had no intention of doing.

Outward-bound, their holds were filled with cotton and tobacco, returning with cargoes of arms and military stores. There was always room for something small, official items such as drugs and medical equipment, and unofficial items such as tea, coffee, perfumes, pins and needles, personally acquired and personally sold—for gold. The captain's profits were great, the stockholders' dividends encouraging, the crew's wages high—and the risks considerable, but they still took them.

Established shipping companies were warned off by the Doctrine of Continuous Voyage, which declared that a prohibited cargo is contraband and liable to seizure from the moment of its original purchase to delivery at its ultimate destination. Calling at an intermediate port for transhipment and resale does not break the continuity of the consignment's journey.

Nassau and Bermuda were the principal points of departure for blockade runners, bound for the Southern States and across the Atlantic. They left in fairly close sequence, so that the pursuit of one would provide covering diversion for the others, using fog or storm to slide through a ring of Yankee cruisers watching just out of range of Confederate shore batteries. As the war went on, ships and crews became tired and strained, but still they took one more gamble, until shells and cannonballs splintered hulls and lacerated men. Even when they docked safely, distribution beyond the confines of the port could be hampered by Northern siege. Only the tiniest quantities of material, such as quinine or salt, could be got through, secreted in the clothes and on the persons of men and women. The personal qualities required by the lawful blockade runners of wartime were not so very different from those of lawbreaking smugglers—ingenuity, self-confidence, a cool head, and a gambler's readiness to hazard all past advantage on a single throw. The Confederate blockade runners of the American Civil War kept risking their ships, their lives and fortunes until the very end of the conflict, their daring immortalized in the character of Rhett Butler in Margaret Mitchell's novel, *Gone with the Wind*.

In no campaign was the strategic weapon of naval blockade apparently more decisive than during World War I. Hemmed in by the Grand Fleet in the North Sea, Germany was cut off from the products of her newly acquired colonies, while her factories could not export those manufactured goods which purchased food and raw materials from overseas. German industry became skilful at producing nourishment from artificial substances and equipment from unorthodox materials, but the cut-off from natural sources was too abrupt and these expediencies could not be improvised in a hurry. Quantity was more important than quality and *ersatz* came to mean 'inferior,' not just 'substitute.'

In an attempt to counteract the 'Baby Starvers,' as the Royal Navy was called in Germany, the undersea merchant ship *Deutschland* was built. Although unorthodox, she had a civilian crew and a mercantile master, and could carry a cargo of 750 tons. She made two journeys to the United States, her crew being given a heroes' welcome on their return. Her sister *Bremen* was lost with all hands on her maiden voyage, while a third ship, *Oldenburg*, was due for completion in 1917. Five more were under construction, but the quantities they could carry were so small compared with the demands of industry and the hunger of the population. And when the United States entered the war, there were no longer any ports to which any Central Powers' ship—surface or submersible—could go. *Deutschland* and her sisters were converted or completed as conventional long-range U-boats with torpedoes and guns.

The British Isles were even more dependent upon imports than the German Empire. Already unrestricted submarine warfare was strangling the British people. But, in the end, the convoys were fought through in a series of minuscule three-dimensional battles. The U-boats were defeated, the battleships of the Grand Fleet reigned supreme on the surface, and the blockade of Germany was as instrumental as the Allied armies in the subjection of the Central Powers.

And so, just eighteen years later, when war with Germany again seemed a possibility, the British government began giving serious thought to the weapon of blockade. It was hoped that the resulting shortages would again cause the breakdown of the German economy and the rebellion of the German people— just as had happened in World War I. However, that same conflict had also shown that modern weapons now prevented the enforcement of a close blockade with warships off every one of the enemy's ports. So, by 1939, a distant blockade was envisaged, for sealing off the approaches to the North Sea from Scapa Flow and the Channel bases.

Strictly speaking, this remote surveillance could not legally be termed a blockade, according to traditional definitions. With this sort of argument in mind, the British government decided to forestall at least one cause for complaint. On 3 September 1939, it announced that the authority responsible for waging this campaign would be formally designated the Ministry of Economic Warfare, under Ronald Cross (later followed by Hugh Dalton and then Lord Selborne). The Admiralty section dealing with contraband control at sea was named the Economic Warfare Division. Its Director was Rear-Admiral A.H. Taylor, later succeeded by Captain O.E. Hallifax. The use of this term 'economic warfare' rather than 'blockade' also reflected the diverse measures to be employed. The interception of enemy merchant vessels and cargoes was only the most obvious and most publicized.

Outside neutral territorial waters, a belligerent warship had—and still has— the right to call upon any merchant ship of any nation to stop. This order is given by recognizable means of communication. If ignored, it can be emphasized by a shot across the bows and then one over the ship. The merchantman must submit to a visit by a boarding party, and examination of her papers, a search of her cargo and an interrogation of her passengers and crew. This must never be done inside neutral territorial waters, where every merchant ship (including any belligerent), but no warship, has right of innocent passage. Stopping and searching must be done without diverting or unreasonably delaying the merchant vessel. This is often impracticable in the open sea, so ships are then directed to examination centres.

Naturally there are neutral objections to this extra voyaging with its attendant delay and cost, and which may also take the merchantman into a hazardous zone. The belligerent's reply is that it is far more dangerous to heave-to where hostile submarines are operating, while an inspecting officer spends hours, perhaps days, going through capacious holds and a maze of tiny compartments, and then establishing exactly where the cargo is going in accordance with the Doctrine of Continuous Voyage. Besides, it might be too rough or too foggy to send a boat across. In any case, at the examination centre, the neutral master will be supplied with approximate locations of minefields, both friendly and—when known—enemy, plus other up-to-date navigational information. Failure to obtain such details may result in refusal of insurance cover. Neutral shipowners who are persistently unco-operative may find it difficult to fuel when they next call at one of the belligerent's ports. But nobody wants awkward problems like that. Governments, neutral and belligerent, come to their various agreements usually before such situations arise, and instruct their nationals accordingly.

When inspected at an examination centre or on the high seas, the neutral vessel may be found to be carrying contraband (what the belligerent has declared to be forbidden articles) to the enemy. Then her cargo and passengers can be detained, and perhaps the ship as well. If the merchantman be enemy (and in this case she will certainly have been stopped on the high seas), ship, cargo and personnel (wherever their destination) are provisionally seized subject to condemnation by prize court. Personal effects are sacrosanct and are not to be stolen from their owners. Items officially removed for service use must be valued and a compensatory payment made to the Prize Marshal.

During World War II the AMC (armed merchant cruiser) *California* acquired from one captured vessel several sextants (only one had been issued during conversion), a bell (for presentation to a museum), perishable provisions (for crew consumption) and sundry equipment (for evaluation by naval intelligence). All these things had to be paid for out the captain's pocket, the ship's funds and the Admiralty's budget.

Those World War II sailors who hoped to make a fortune out of prize money were sadly disappointed. When captured ships were sold, their value was shared between all members of the Royal Navy, whether present or not. It was argued that everybody, including shorebased personnel, helped intercept the enemy, and so RAF Coastal Command was entitled to a share as well. The whole business was abolished after 1945.

If the captured prize is to be sailed to a port, her mercantile crew must co-operate with the warship's boarding party. They will not be prisoners of war, but civilian internees, a distinction not always apparent to the captives. If the prize is to be sunk because it is not possible to get her to port, then the warship must first ensure that the merchant seamen and the ship's papers are in a safe place—and that excludes lifeboats in the middle of the ocean.

Submarines and aircraft are thus apparently useless as commerce raiders. Either they cannot succour the survivors (which they must legally do) or they must sacrifice their advantages of invisibility and speed. However, if the merchantman offers any resistance at all, the intercepting warship can open fire without warning, and continue shooting until the captain considers resistance has ceased. Failing to stop can be interpreted as resistance, and so can calling for help or broadcasting the ship's position. Employing defensive armament or proceeding in convoy, sailing in a declared prohibited area (which might be an entire ocean), refusing to co-operate with the boarding party, or even removing the ship's papers can all count as resistance.

All merchant seamen in war are aware that they can find themselves in any of these situations at any time, but for those who are sailing alone on a hostile sea and likely to be intercepted—the lot of all blockade runners—there is an additional hazard. Obviously their cargo must be of exceptional value and importance, otherwise they would not be running such risks; it must not fall into enemy hands. But scuttling when ordered not to is yet another interpretation of resistance. Even further, it can be alleged that the merchant seamen have abandoned ship voluntarily, are not technically survivors, and need not be rescued. Indeed, some international jurists argue that they can be fired on until they return to their ship and halt the scuttling process that only they know about.

As he goes over the side into the water, every wartime survivor wonders what treatment the potential captor will mete out; blockade runners have more to think about than most.

Germany's leaders were as aware as the British government of the significance of blockade. Self-sufficiency was one of the great goals of the NSDAP (the Nazi party). It would free the economy of the Third Reich from the threat of outside interference and enhance Aryan dignity. They came nearest to achieving this aim in food production, 83 per cent of requirements being met on German soil. $14\frac{1}{2}$ per cent was imported over the frontiers of neighbouring states, future supply from these sources being assured by subsequent invasion. By September 1939, only $2\frac{1}{2}$ per cent of Germany's food was being delivered by sea, but that amount included certain edible oils and solid fats which could not be produced in the homeland.

Industrial independence was more difficult; manufacturing nations are not always favoured by natural resources. Remembering their expediencies of World War I, German chemists set out to improve the techniques of substitution and invent new ones. During that earlier conflict, Germany had been cut off from Chilean nitrates without which no modern explosives or fertilizers can be made. Then I.G. Farbenindustrie had synthesized nitrates from air. In the 1930s artificial rubber became one of their most successful projects. It was made from *butadiene* (a highly inflammable gas) and *natrium* (or sodium) and hence was called buna. By August 1939, German plants were turning out 25,000 tons a year. Other countries were interested, particularly the United States, whose Standard Oil Company exchanged information with I.G. Farben. Research by the English was minimal, as they had easy access to rubber plantations in Malaya.

Oil was another natural product denied Germany, but available to her potential enemies. Not only was it a vital fuel, but its constituent elements were important ingredients in the very synthetics which German scientists were trying to develop. Trainloads of tank cars trundled across Europe from the oilfields and refineries of co-operative countries such as the Soviet Union and Romania, but it was not enough. This substance also had to be made artificially in Germany, mainly from coal and shale. Three million tons a year were being produced by 1939, giving Adolf Hitler fuel reserves for six months of war.

That might be enough for a swift Polish campaign—provided no other state intervened. It was obviously not enough for a lengthy total war involving worldwide operations. It was anticipated that such a conflict would commence in the mid-1940s. By then German industry would have made and amassed all the *matériel* needed by a great war machine. Some things could not be produced artificially—at any rate not as technology was then. The list included tin, wolfram, whale oil, fish products, wood pulp and bauxite. Even the steel industry, one of Germany's traditional strengths, annually imported 22,000,000 tons.

So stockpiles of these overseas materials would have to be built up, a process which had been going on since 1933, when Hitler had become Chancellor with Dr Hjalmar Horace Greeley Schacht as his economics expert. German merchant vessels were to be engaged in this traffic until the very outbreak of war. To have ceased trading too early during a carefully engineered crisis would arouse the suspicions of potential enemies, especially Britain. If some ships were still at sea when war did come, there was just a possibility that one or two would evade the Royal Navy, adding their quotas to Germany's strategic reserves. It was a risk they would have to take, just as der Führer was risking a ruinous war while hoping for a series of successful lightning campaigns or bloodless coups.

Germany's merchant service could not expect much comfort from the Kriegsmarine in the event of war. There was no suggestion that *panzerschiffe* (pocket battleships), cruisers and destroyers should go out to South American, East African or Asiatic waters to escort convoys home. The best that could be hoped was for warships to distract or damage the Royal Navy to cover the return of a few merchantmen in the North Atlantic. The protection of world-wide trade was not one of the Kriegsmarine's major functions as it was for the Royal Navy. Indeed, the priority of the relationship was reversed; it was the wartime role of the merchant marine to support oceanic operations conducted by the Kriegsmarine which was itself subject to the military requirements of the Wehrmacht.

It was not easy to make any prewar arrangements for co-operation between the navy and mercantile marine. The usual differences between civilian and military seafarers had been exacerbated by the Treaty of Versailles which declared that no officer or man of the German mercantile marine should receive any training in the navy. Even if such links had not been expressly forbidden by outside agency, it is unlikely that they would have found much favour amongst German shipowners of independent mind. They wanted Germany to have a merchant fleet of world importance, but they wanted to achieve eminence by being efficient carriers, not through depending upon government subsidy, with all the bureaucratic interference that would entail. Of course, under the Nazi regime, everything had to be organized and so all German shipping companies, fishermen, agents, port constructors and operators, navigation authorities and lifeboats, were brought together in the Reichsverkehrsgruppe Seeschifffahrt. Its director was the go-ahead chairman of the German Shipowners Association, John T. Essberger. He tried to ensure that the organization fulfilled the same role as similar combinations in democratic countries, namely the encouragement of business and professional activities, not the promotion of political beliefs. In particular, he insisted that seagoing transport was essentially free-trade internationalism, not an industry which could be incorporated into the insulated economy of a self-sufficient state. Attempts to restrict traffic to the German flag only, would result in reprisal navigation acts, hindering the Reich's stockpiling programme and preventing German merchantmen from earning foreign currency by acting as general carriers.

This independent attitude was maintained during the war. The Kriegsmarine (and the Wehrmacht) could requisition and charter merchant ships, it could direct their cargoes and their routes, but it did not absorb or completely control the mercantile marine in the same way as the Admiralty's Trade Division assumed operational responsibility for the Merchant Navy of the British Empire. Instead Reichsverkehrsgruppe Seeschifffahrt was expected to co-operate with the requirements of the Kriegsmarine, who in turn would take what steps where necessary for the protection of mercantile movements. Kriegsmarinedienstellen (Navy Service Offices—KMD) were set up in Hamburg, Bremen and Stettin and Königsberg, with others being opened in other ports as the war developed. Responsible for organizing the voyages of logistic transports and commercial carriers within their area, they were more liaison than commanding authorities, transmitting instructions by means of conferences with individual masters, who could refer controversial matters back to their respective companies.

There were no KMD abroad but before the war German Intelligence (Abwehr) and the Kriegsmarine had together and in co-operation with the Economics Ministry (Wirtschaftsministerium), established a clandestine Emergency Naval Supply Service (Marinesonderdienst—MSD). Obviously it had to be secret to prevent enemy knowledge of German plans, but also it had to avoid embarrassing friendly neutrals.

Such countries can trade with belligerents if they are prepared to risk losing cargoes, ships and men. They are not allowed to permit their soil to be used as a base for belligerent warships or for any other warlike activity. Even if this biased participation does not warrant military retaliation, the less-favoured belligerent can employ a variety of diplomatic and economic pressures.

So, overseas agents of German shipping companies received routine and social visits from naval attachés and officers from warships on peacetime cruises. Instruction and codes were transferred and locked away in company and consular strongrooms. Mixed in with the everyday transactions of a shipping line would be the purchase of naval supplies and fuel. These were stored in preparation either for the direct delivery of diesel to U-boats in sympathetic neutral harbours or for the wartime loading of German merchantmen and their despatch as supply vessels for surface and submarine raiders. The balance of their cargo would be made up of strategic raw material for onward transit to Germany. Any inquisitive observer could never be quite sure from her cargo whether she was intended as a naval auxiliary or as a commercial blockade runner, thus depriving the Royal Navy of clues about the location of disguised raiders. No one could anticipate which vessels would be able to reach the security of neutral harbours at the outbreak of war nor which of those would be suitable. Those selected would be informed by the local German representative, who would hand over the items entrusted to him. Masters would be given further orders by SKL A.VI Schifffahrtsabteilung (the Merchant Ship Section of Seekriegsleitung —the Kriegsmarine's Operations Division). Signals were broadcast at specific times, the messages being padded out to standard length by coded poetry or meaningless groups of letters and figures. The supply ships and blockade runners normally maintained the strictest radio silence, although a special zip code enabled a considerable amount of basic information to be transmitted in a few seconds. It was normally used by raiders to report their successes and intentions.

Vessels leaving German-controlled ports in wartime usually had a Kriegsmarine officer and ratings on board, sometimes as passengers and sometimes to man the ship's defensive armament. In theory, the senior Kriegsmarine officer was in charge of the ship, but German masters always insisted that, according to hallowed maritime tradition, they, and they alone, were responsible under God for the safety of the ship, passengers, cargo and crew.

All German merchant seamen belonged to the single state-controlled trade union, Deutsche Arbeitsfront, but few were members of the NSDAP. At least one member of each crew was expected to maintain the zeal of his comrades, efforts which met with the same response as any political or religious activity in any ship of any nation; it all depended on personal enthusiasm. A very small minority were Gestapo agents, ready to report on the reliability of their superiors. Such men could make a ship very unhappy, but their numbers were probably much less than was believed. British interrogators were always on the lookout for Gestapo agents and some did carry evidence of this, while others seem to have been innocent but bad-tempered loners.

On several occasions during the war, Grossadmiral Raeder and Grossadmiral Dönitz both demanded that the German merchant marine be brought completely under naval control, but it always remained independent of the

Kriegsmarine although in 1944 the latter absorbed the Marinesonderdienst from the Abwehr and the Economics Ministry.

In 1942, the merchant navy was itself brought more closely together under a Reichskommissar Seeschifffahrt, by which time it was intended to integrate the European coastal trade with all Germany's transport. The Reichskommissar was directly responsible to Hitler, who was always content to keep related organizations separate from and slightly jealous of each other. The whole atmosphere surrounding the operation of Germany's merchant fleet during World War II contained the seeds of discord and confusion, but like most such situations, the practical people involved in its day-to-day running made the system work much better than might have been expected.

Not that, back in 1939, there was much the Kriegsmarine and mercantile marine could do except agree to co-operate. There were no common signal books or steaming diagrams for mixed groups of warships and merchantmen. The latter used latitude and longitude to report their positions, while Kriegsmarine operations were plotted on alpha-numerical charts. The Kriegsmarine did not even have enough surplus navigational charts to issue relevant sets to all masters. Merchant vessels usually keep to a fairly predictable route and timetable and rarely carry large-scale charts and sailing instructions for other parts of the world. If the master could obtain them from some other source, who would pay for them or for blackout material or the paint used to camouflage the ship? Such problems were encountered by all merchant navies as World War II approached, its onset naturally viewed with more apprehension by ocean-going masters and crews than by those engaged in coastal or riverine trade.

3 The Luck of the Game

In the early hours of 25 August 1939, Norddeich Radio despatched Telegram QWA7 to all 2466 German merchantmen. It was a warning that war was imminent. The sealed Sonderanweisung für Handelsschiffe (Special Instructions for Merchant Ships which included Secret Code 'H' for 'Handelsschifffahrt') reposing in every master's safe, were to be opened, read and acted upon. They were ordered to foresake their normal routes immediately and keep at least 30 to 100 miles away from the main shipping lanes. QWA8 instructed all captains to disguise their ships and make for Germany, avoiding the English Channel. QWA8 was signed 'Essberger,' but QWA9 on 27 August came from Marineleitung. It told all German ships to reach home, friendly or neutral ports within the next four days. Spanish, Italian, Japanese, Russian and Dutch harbours were preferable. The United States should only be visited in an emergency. In QWA10, OKM (the German admiralty) raised the four-day limit and ordered as many captains as possible to get home, either now or in the following month. It was now obvious that this crisis was more than a Baltic or Central European affair. There was only one enemy that could threaten Germany's merchant ships wherever they were—the Royal Navy.

The atmosphere of doubtful unreality was dispelled by QWA11 on 3 September 1939, followed by QWA12. Great Britain and France had declared war on Germany. Ships should only attempt to pass between the Shetlands and Norway in dark or foggy weather. Now, at this very moment, in the mists of the North Atlantic, under sunny southern skies, in the starry Pacific night, the Royal Navy would be out looking for isolated German merchantmen—would be out looking for *them*.

Their fears were well grounded. British warships were indeed at sea and had been for several days, making towards or already patrolling off the great focal points of the world's trade routes. One such was the Tribal-class destroyer *Somali*, leader of the 6th Destroyer Flotilla and engaged in screening ships of the

Home Fleet some 350 miles to the south of Iceland. About two hours after the declaration of war, lookouts sighted a three-island cargo vessel on the horizon. As Captain Gresham Nicholson steered *Somali* to investigate and challenge her, it was seen that the stranger was wearing the German ensign, but her crew had apparently been trying to paint out her name. *Somali* put a party on board to learn that she was the German *Hanna Böge*, owned by Johann M.K. Blumenthal of Hamburg. Her master was Kapitän Christiansen, nearly sixty years old, and a native of Schleswig-Holstein. *Hanna Böge* was clean and comfortable and had been completed by Neptunwerft of Rostock in 1938. Her 1100-hp steam engine gave the 2377-ton ship a speed of 10 knots. Her modern bridge equipment included a revolution indicator and other instruments to aid station-keeping. The boarding officer wondered if she had been designed with fleet work in mind.

Hanna Böge normally traded between Nova Scotia and Germany, and she was now returning with a cargo of wood pulp. It filled the holds and was even stowed on deck, its total value being estimated at £1,000,000. Quite apart from its monetary worth, wood pulp was a necessary ingredient in the manufacture of military handbooks, documents and maps, in the production of cardboard for fuzes, and in the preparation of explosives. She was an enemy ship, carrying strategic raw material to the enemy, but her crew had offered no resistance, so Captain Nicholson would not be justified in sinking her without further ado. Nor indeed had he any wish to do so. Her acquisition would not only deny the enemy a fine modern vessel and her cargo, but would augment the Allied war effort by an equivalent measure.

Kapitän Christiansen and his twenty officers and men were naturally perturbed at not being able to get home, but otherwise they were friendly and co-operated with the prize crew put on board their ship. This consisted of Lieutenant-Commander Seymour Tuke (*Somali*'s First Lieutenant), eight ratings and a telegraphist. The composition of boarding parties was usually left to the discretion of captains and first lieutenants in the early days of the war. Sometimes officers and ratings were detailed, but in some ships, particularly those with large complements which were more likely to have spare hands, volunteers were called for from various branches. Their training too was individualistic. There was little guidance in the peacetime Navy concerning the best method of boarding a ship on the high seas in the face of armed resistance, or what to do about passive resistance, how to identify contraband, where to look for explosive charges in a strange ship, how to deal with damage once it had occurred, or what documents and portable equipment to grab and escape with if the merchantman were going down fast. Some captains, enthusiasts for this form of warfare, were able to prepare their boarding parties for such eventualities, and included personnel with mercantile experience. In other ships, newly commissioned and still working up, or fully engaged twenty-four hours a day in other tasks, there was no opportunity to muster the boarding party before a suspicious merchant-man hove in sight. Then all depended upon the general experience and adapt-ability of the regular officers and ratings involved.

Hanna Böge parted company from *Somali* at 6.30 pm, heading due east for the Pentland Firth some 600 miles away. That night a W/T signal told of the sinking of the liner *Athenia*, about 100 miles south of their track. For a while the Britons on *Hanna Böge* wondered if the U-boat would make for them, taking revenge on the Royal Navy's first high seas prize of World War II. Nothing happened and *Hanna Böge* arrived at Kirkwall in the Orkneys on 5 September, in time for her prize crew to return to *Somali* when she came in from patrol. *Hanna Böge* was renamed *Crown Arun* and was eventually torpedoed off Ireland a year later.

The German crews of seized merchantmen were sent to internment camps. Few seemed to know whether they would be paid during their imprisonment and some were quite worried because they had heard that such camps were run by Jews, and either feared racial contamination or reprisal. In the early months of the war, the common experience of running an unarmed ship through hazardous seas could result in a wary comradeship and an exchange of home addresses between boarding party and German crew, especially former residents of the United States. Later some relatives of Royal Navy personnel corresponded with German internees. One such letter, opened by censor and dated 30 Novem-ber 1939 (not from a member of *Hanna Böge*'s crew) read:

> Dear Madam, I received your friendly letter and was very glad to hear that Georg is well. It has been the first sign from the outside world since my internment. I will never forget the day of our capture when fate send us friends instead enemys. and I believe if your and my people knew mor of each other this war would be impossible. But now we must be patient and pray for peace. I have not had any news from my people so they do not know about my whereabout. My internment is not quit so bad. I get to share my room with 2 shipmates. The house is steamheated and every floor has 4 bathtubs. This is very comfortable. The most beautiful spot to me is a lawn before the building surrounded by hedges and rosebushes, and in the background hills. I am not allowed to write more than 12 lines according to camprules so I must end this letter. If it is not to much to ask of you, would you please send me some toothpaste, and somethin to smoke and a few magazines or old books? My greetings to George. Can he not write to me? I would sure like to hear from him. Ever your grateful, Wilhelm.

It was now a matter of sheer chance whether a German merchantman was berthed in a German, friendly, neutral or hostile port, was close to home, just outside territorial waters, inside a British patrol area, or well placed but short of fuel. The crews whose ships were intercepted could only accept their fate with resignation, although that did not mean that they awaited it passively, for they had already received orders to deny enemy possession. As the White Ensign appeared over the horizon or a group of uniformed men came along the quay-side, many masters and men tried to make some use of their last minutes of freedom. Wireless sets were wrecked, important documents destroyed and navigation equipment slighted. The ship's engines were too massive for amateur saboteurs to injure, but gauges and controls could be smashed. Greatest harm could be done by attacking the system of pipes which drew salt water from outside the hull, circulated it through the condensers to cool fresh boiler feed-water, and then returned it to the sea. The pump was stopped, the pipe fractured on the inboard side, and the pump restarted. Meanwhile other valves such as those used for flooding the holds in case of fire were opened, certain parts being disconnected and thrown into the bilges where they would soon be concealed by corrosive seawater. As the chief engineer escaped up the ladders, he could see the ocean gushing around machinery and lapping floor plates, some of which had been taken up to trip unwary strangers.

But all this destruction took time. It was simple to crack a few panes of glass, but that did not affect a ship's seaworthiness. Covers and panels had to be unbolted to get at really vital pieces of equipment. Fire seemed an obvious weapon, but an impromptu blaze which the arsonist could easily escape could also be speedily extinguished by a boarding party. And which documents should be destroyed? The H Code, yes, but what about navigation charts, tables, company correspondence? Masters and officers had spent their lives keeping daily logs, recording every event and transaction and signal, looking after cargo manifests, receipts, insurance certificates, passports and paybooks. They did not want to annihilate all that documentation—which might be required quite normally again tomorrow. Even if they did, how could they be certain of destroying or rendering illegible a quantity of paper equivalent to a shelfful of telephone directories. It was impossible to tear it all up. Thrown overboard it would float long enough to be recovered and dried out. Burning (except several decks down in the furnaces—which motor vessels do not have) would only char the edges. No, the documents must first be sorted out.

Only the master could do that. Only the master could arrange their destruction. Only the master could decide what had to be done about scuttling, surrender, abandoning ship. As in all navies, military and civilian, only the captain could decide what had to be done about anything. Without orders, no deckhand or greaser could start smashing things or throwing them overboard. And perhaps the master was ashore or asleep, the sort of man whose waking temper was more to be feared than any hostile gunfire. Perhaps he was of humane character, unwilling to risk his men's lives in open boats upon a stormy sea. Perhaps he had passengers and had spent his career putting their safety and comfort first. Perhaps some of his crew were neutrals. Perhaps he did not believe that there was going to be a war after all, just something like the Sudeten crisis the previous year. Perhaps he thought he could outrun that distant cruiser or fool that boarding officer. Perhaps through some communications breakdown he did not know that war was imminent. Perhaps he knew that scuttling was an infringement of the Rules of War, and he did not want his crew to be fired on. And why wreck a perfectly good ship, when as loyal Germans, they knew it would be returned with their country's victory in a couple of months' time?

Even if they were prepared to prevent anything falling temporarily into British hands, they would, as seamen, be reluctant to inflict pain on any part of the floating home that they had cherished and relied upon for so long. They were civilian merchant seamen who wanted to mind their own business, not ocean-going warriors, eager for battle and glory. It took a little while for them to adjust to the new conditions of wartime.

Some adjusted very quickly, or were already prepared for trouble. Both *Carl Fritzen* and *Olinda* scuttled themselves when found by the cruiser *Ajax* between Rio Grande do Sul and the River Plate on the first and second days of the war. The 6594-ton *Carl Fritzen* was an old tramp steamer proceeding in ballast, while *Olinda* (of 4576 tons) was more modern and was believed to be carrying iron and cotton. In both instances the crew were saved and the foundering hulks finished off with 4-inch (10.2-cm) gunfire. Some of the merchant seamen promised not to participate in the war and were transferred to the tanker *San Gerardo* to be landed in Montevideo.

On the other side of the Atlantic, another crew was having to react quickly to the outbreak of hostilities. The 5042-ton *Togo* belonged to the Woermann Linie, part of the Deutsche Afrika Linien consortium. She was at Douala in the Cameroons, a former German colony which was now administered by French mandate. She managed to get clear of the estuary before a French warship could arrive, her 6100-hp diesel taking her down the coast at 16 knots. Kapitän Rouffelet passed French Equatorial Africa without interception and entered the mouth of the River Congo, secure in Belgian neutrality until ready to make a dash for home.

Erlangen's crew displayed even more ingenuity and were rewarded with incredible luck. This 6101-ton Norddeutscher Lloyd freighter was at Timaru on South Island, New Zealand, in August 1939. Close by was berthed the armed trawler *Wakakura*, but apart from cursory observation, the New Zealanders took no interest in the German vessel. *Erlangen* called at Dunedin and then made for New South Wales; a bunker full of Australian coal would be sufficient to get her to Germany. War was declared while still on route to the coaling station, so a wireless message ordered her to Chile. Unfortunately she did not have enough fuel to attain even that neutral haven. Alone, on the far side of the world—no crew could have been farther from home—her master steered for Auckland Island, 300 miles southwest of New Zealand. Uninhabited and located in the path of the prevailing westerlies, the island had sheltered German whalers on previous occasions. In fact the New Zealand cruiser *Leander* had already visited the place looking for just such vessels. *Erlangen* entered Carnley Harbour and nosed into the innermost creek of the mountain-sided straits and inlets separating Auckland and Adams Islands. *Erlangen* was named after a Bavarian town, but the verb *erlangen* means 'to obtain,' and that is what her crew did. They went ashore, chopping down trees and cutting them into suitable lengths for the ship's stokehole at the rate of 20 tons a day. It was fortunate that *Erlangen* was coalburning, and not oilfired, especially not a diesel motor vessel. Now came *Leander* again. The New Zealand authorities suspected this remote island and its distant neighbour, Campbell Island. If German vessels (merchantmen, pocket battleships, U-boat tankers—all sorts of rumours were current and believed in those early weeks) were lurking somewhere near the Antipodean shipping lanes, what better place than these isolated islands.

Leander dropped anchor in Carnley Harbour itself, sending out her boats to examine every inlet radiating from the main sound. The weather was cold and so bad that the cruiser's Supermarine Walrus could not be used for aerial reconnaissance. Then *Leander* was ordered back to New Zealand. She departed forthwith, leaving some of the wooded creeks still unexplored. One of them secreted *Erlangen*.

That missed booty was small compared with the greatest prize of all, another NDL vessel being sought in the North Atlantic. Ever since 31 August, the British Home Fleet had been hoping to catch the Blue Riband liner *Bremen*. Her 51,731 tons made her the largest ship in German service and the third largest in the world. She had sailed from Bremerhaven on 22 August, made her usual calls and was in mid-Atlantic when the war warnings started to come in. Kapitän Ahrens decided to proceed, arriving in New York on the evening of 28 August to disembark his passengers, including Britons. The ship turned around in quick time, but now the harbour authorities insisted on inspecting her thoroughly, naturally taking their proper rest periods and meal breaks. No weapons were found; her lifeboats met statutory requirements and could be raised and lowered satisfactorily. A list was even made of all the lifejackets on board. Not that *Bremen* would be carryng any of her 2232 passengers, only the 1013 crew-members. The New York authorities were completely justified in ensuring that safety precautions in all likely belligerent ships leaving American shores in time of crisis were up to standard, but it did seem to *Bremen*'s officers that President Roosevelt was deliberately trying to delay the liner until British patrols could be in an intercepting position. Perhaps, they reasoned, the Americans were hoping that Kapitän Ahrens would not dare to leave harbour and that *Bremen* might be eventually seized for the US merchant marine; they were not far wrong.

But *Bremen*'s crew were confident, probably the most confident of all Germany's merchant seamen at that time; confident of their immediate future and of the eventual outcome of the conflict. 'Everything from Germany is of the best' was one of their shipboard sayings. It was their duty to preserve *Bremen* for the time when she would again be Queen of the North Atlantic. Their confidence in their ship was justified. Back in 1929 she had gained the Blue Riband at 27.83 knots. She was still fast, perhaps rather faster than the Royal Navy expected a merchant ship to be—in spite of all the publicity.

Bremen departed New York on 30 August, leaving North American waters before any cruisers were in position. At 28 knots she sped northeastwards through heavy, but lessening, seas and thick fog. On 3 September 1939, she was south of the latitude of Iceland, entering the Denmark Strait, while five British battleships, two battlecruisers, one aircraft carrier, twelve cruisers and seventeen destroyers patrolled between Scotland and Iceland. Even though the liner might evade these watchers, the warships sweeping across the North Sea to Norway would block her homeward passage and that of her compatriots who also went northabout around Iceland.

However, *Bremen* was not going to Germany. Blacked out and painted grey (from lifeboats lowered to just above the rushing water), she kept above the Arctic Circle, rounded North Cape and entered Kola Inlet on 6–7 September. There, at Murmansk. in the company of other liners, she rested, guest of Germany's new Russian partner. No war would ever reach these inhospitable parts.

Out in the equatorial East Indies, similar sighs of relief were being breathed by the crew of *Franken* as she slipped through Dutch territorial waters to enter the neutral Sumatran port of Padang. Fairey Swordfish from the carrier *Eagle* observed her passage, but as their quarry kept within—and they had to stay outside—the three-mile limit, they could do nothing—for the moment. But, sooner or later, all those German ships, waiting in neutral or forgotten harbours, wasting time in zigzagging circles in the middle of the ocean, would make a move. Some might only creep or dash towards another safe haven, but sooner or later, they would all make for Germany. Sooner or later, they would all be passing Iceland, north- or southabout, to reach the security of Scandinavian territorial waters. It was to intercept these blockade runners, inspect neutral merchantmen and keep an eye on British independents, that the Northern Patrol was established on 6 September 1939.

4 Contraband Control

Caledon, *Calypso*, *Diomede*, *Dragon*, *Effingham*, *Emerald*, *Cardiff* and *Dunedin* were the original members of the Northern Patrol under Vice-Admiral Sir Max Horton. Ideally, they should have been stationed so that their patrol lines (roughly parallel in an east-west or northeast-southwest direction) were no more than 50 miles apart, and closer in bad weather. In practice three cruisers were always absent at Scapa Flow or Sullum Vöe, fuelling or refitting. This meant that there were rarely more than two in the 200-mile gap between the Shetlands and the Faeroes, the other three covering the 250 miles from the Faeroes to Iceland. Very soon the 200-mile wide Denmark Strait was added to the Patrol's responsibility, although this distance could be reduced by thick ice, even in summer. By then too, the first of fifty-six AMCs (armed merchant cruisers) were entering service.

These were fast liners listed by the Admiralty as suitable for conversion to warships. As soon as hostilities began, they were requisitioned wherever they happened to be berthed. Much of their luxury accommodation was ripped out and unnecessary deck fittings, such as dummy funnels, surplus masts and rows of lifeboats, were removed. Spare guns had been stored at depots around the world since 1918, ready for just such an emergency. They were brought out and hoisted aboard to give AMCs as powerful an armament as the regular cruisers of the Northern Patrol. One of them, the former P & O liner *Corfu* had nine 6-inch (15.2-cm) guns plus a catapult for a reconnaissance seaplane. They ranged in size from the 6267-ton *Bulolo* to *Queen of Bermuda* (of 22,575 tons).

AMCs were quite different from the Defensively Equipped Merchant Ships (DEMS) organization, supplying guns to merchantmen which remained the property of their owners. AMCs were commissioned under the White Ensign as proper warships of the Royal Navy. Many were commanded by officers retired under the Geddes Axe and other economies of the interwar period, but who now returned to service. At first their crews were either recalled reservists or ex-merchant seamen who stayed on in their own ship to man the engines or perform other duties with which they were already familiar. They signed T124X Articles, which enabled them to be paid their higher shipping company rates while coming under uniformed naval discipline. They were also permitted to keep Merchant Navy watches, so that a man on duty from midnight to 4 am, repeated that 'trick' every twelve hours, for the duration of the patrol. Royal Navy personnel were accustomed to Dog Watches from 4 pm to 6pm and 6 pm to 8 pm, so that everybody had a share of the unpleasant watches. The two systems could be operated simultaneously in the same AMC.

There were similar arrangements for manning thirteen armed boarding vessels (ABVs). Apart from Lamport & Holt's *Vandyck* of 13,241 gross tons, ABVs were smaller than AMCs, ranging downwards from *Chantala* (3129 tons) to the 757-ton *Fratton* (formerly a Southern Railway steamer). They mounted a couple of 4-inch (10.2-cm) guns and were intended for employment in more restricted areas, such as the Fair Isle and English Channels. Inshore waters were patrolled by armed trawlers of 500 tons or so, while the requisitioned drifters and yachts of the Examination Service and the Harbour Defence organization covered the approaches to commercial ports and roadsteads. Later on in the war, much of this coastal work was taken over by specially constructed motor-launches and trawlers, the latter also being capable of high seas patrol and escort. Another subsequent development was the ocean boarding vessel (OBV), forming a link between the ABVs and the AMCs. They varied from *Malvernian* to Canadian National's *Lady Somers* (3133 to 8194 gross tons). OBVs' main armament comprised two 6-inch (15.2-cm) guns. At least one, *Hilary*, boasted an anti-aircraft kite and four Harvey Projectors, launching a 9-foot rocket with a fearsome rearward blast. These were manned by a Royal Artillery sergeant and eight men. *Hilary*'s routine was typical of that performed by OBVs. Based at Greenock, she accompanied a convoy until the ships were dispersed in mid-Atlantic. She then remained on patrol in the southwestern approaches, for as long as three weeks before meeting and helping to escort a UK-bound convoy.

All these types of improvised warship found worldwide employment but they were soonest in service around the British Isles, the AMCs being concentrated on the Northern Patrol. A certain amount of co-operation came from eighteen biplane flying boats based in northern Britain, each of which could, in theory, cover a beat of 300 miles or more. Of greater comfort to the old cruisers and AMCs was their occasional reinforcement by newer, more armoured Counties and Towns with their modern 8-inch and 6-inch (20.3-cm and 15.2-cm) armament. Distant cover was provided by the capital ships of the Home Fleet at Scapa Flow, ready to head off any German warships trying to break out into the Atlantic or protect returning blockade runners. The Royal Navy's AMCs were not intended for full-scale combat against battlecruisers and *panzerschiffe*, not even against disguised raiders, seemingly opponents of similar metal. The AMCs were given just enough firepower to overawe defenceless or lightly armed merchantmen. Their function was the denial of strategic material to the enemy, whether in belligerent or neutral bottoms.

A list of forbidden items of possible value to the German war effort had been issued by the Ministry of Economic Warfare on 4 September 1939. It ran as follows (quoted from Stubbs, *The Navy at War*):

a) All kinds of arms, ammunition, explosives, chemicals or appliances suitable for use in chemical warfare and machines for their manufacture and repair; component parts thereof; articles necessary or convenient for their use; materials or ingredients used in their manufacture; articles necessary or convenient for the production or use of such materials or ingredients.

b) Fuel of all kinds; all contrivances for, or means of transportation on land, in the water or air, and machines used in their manufacture or repair; component parts thereof; instruments, articles or animals necessary or convenient for their use; materials or ingredients used in their manufacture; articles necessary or convenient for the production or use of such materials or ingredients.

c) All means of communication, tools, implements, instruments, maps, pictures, and other articles, machines or documents necessary or convenient for carrying on hostile operations; articles necessary or convenient for their manufacture or use.

d) Coin, bullion, currency, evidences of debt; also metal materials, dies, plates, machinery or other articles necessary or convenient for their manufacture.

e) All kinds of food, foodstuffs, forage and clothing, and articles and materials used in their production.

At first this definition of contraband referred only to German imports, but in November 1939 it was extended to German exports, as retaliation for German minelaying in breach of international regulations. This list covered virtually everything of use to a modern state in peacetime, let alone one trying to engage in warlike operations. It was even suggested that a shipload of Bibles could be contraband, as the Scriptures could be pulped down and turned into packing for ammunition.

Bearing this list—his party was not usually armed unless hostility was expected, and even then the weapons were often unloaded in case of accidents— the boarding officer was taken over to the stopped merchantman. If the ship was enemy, all sorts of things might happen as he scrambled up a jumping ladder hung over the side. In most cases she was neutral and nothing dramatic occurred. A couple of ratings remained on guard at the top of the ladder, while a petty officer and junior rates went up to the bridge.

In the master's cabin, perhaps sipping a welcoming drink, the boarding officer examined the cargo manifest, bills of lading, crew and passenger lists, log books and any other papers he thought relevant. All the time he was making conversation, asking questions about the papers, where the ship was going, where she had been, what had been seen. The master's replies varied from eager co-operation to baffled incomprehension and sullen indifference, depending upon the official attitudes adopted by their respective governments, the ability of the two men to speak each other's language, and the master's personal opinion about interfering navalmen who had nothing better to do.

Meanwhile course was being steered towards the nearest examination centre, where the master ought to have presented his ship of his own volition. A list had been promulgated at the same time as the contraband declaration. The earliest were Kirkwall (for the Northern Patrol), Falmouth, Weymouth, Deal (for the Downs), Gibraltar, Malta, Haifa, Port Said and Aden. The French Navy established similar centres at Dunkirk, Oran and Marseilles. The situation at Port Said was rather different, as the Suez Canal Convention had laid down that this channel was an international waterway, so nobody could exercise right of search in the canal, its ports or three miles from it. Accordingly, Royal Navy officers visited masters passing through the canal and—in friendly fashion—pointed out that their ships could either be searched there and receive an appropriate certificate, or they could voluntarily divert to Haifa. If they did neither, they would be stopped three miles out and be taken to Haifa under armed guard.

On anchoring at the examination centre, the boarding party was replaced by a shorebased search party, consisting of several examination officers, usually members of the Royal Naval Reserve with mercantile experience. Backed up by a number of ratings, one officer had the hatches opened up and inspected the cargo. Another checked each member of the crew against his papers, while other officers interviewed every passenger on board. Yet another team went into all the cabins, machinery spaces and store rooms. Meanwhile the ship's papers, already scrutinized at sea, were taken ashore to the manifest office. Again the master was questioned about everything until the most compliant of personalities became irritated and impatient. And all the time, the cost of running machinery and paying the crew's wages was mounting up. If anything were found amiss,—a deckhand with unusual knowledge of naval procedure, a small packet of industrial diamonds in a passenger's luggage, a consignment of rubber for a neutral company with trading subsidiaries in Germany—then the ship was detained, while all the relevant information was relayed to the Contraband Committee in London. Liaising with the Ministère de Blocus (first under Georges Pernot and then Georges Monnet), this body undertook its own investigation, despatching telegrams to naval and commercial agents in the appropriate countries.

Depending upon their replies and upon Allied relations with those neutrals, the Contraband Committee (headed by Lord Justice Finlay) decided what should be done about the matter—whether one man, or one item, or the entire cargo, or the whole ship, should be arrested—or whether, as in most cases, the vessel could be allowed to proceed without further hindrance. Then all the papers were returned and navigation information imparted. A special signal to be displayed by flag hoist when leaving harbour was handed over. If this signal were not flown correctly, the merchantman would be prevented from leaving the roadstead by the duty guardship, a rather grandiose title for what was often an old yacht mounting a single machine-gun of uncertain reliability. A second flag signal was hoisted if intercepted yet again on the high seas to indicate that the merchantman had already been cleared for contraband and need not go through the whole performance again.

In a typical week at just one examination centre early in the war, 131 merchantmen came in, about half proceeding thither voluntarily. Another seventy-four ships were awaiting decisions from previous inspection. By the end of that week, one entire cargo had been seized, together with portions of another twenty shipments. These latter vessels had then been allowed to proceed with the rest of their loads intact. A hundred and fourteen had been released without any confiscation whatsoever, while the remaining ships were awaiting further investigation, which could take up to a fortnight.

While British cruisers and AMCs sought out neutral and German merchantmen in the North Atlantic, French submarines were watching the routes from Spain, the Caribbean and central Atlantic islands. On 28 September, *Poncelet*'s usual routine of surface patrol and practice dives was interrupted when a 5522-ton merchant ship was sighted. The distant vessel made off at 13 knots. The weather was quite good, with hardly any sea. *Poncelet* could do nearly 20 knots on the surface and the stranger was soon within range of the submarine's 100-mm (3.9-inch) gun. The chase continued without a shot being fired until *Poncelet* was in a good torpedo firing position; Lieutenant de Vaisseau (Lieutenant) Bertrand de Saussine wanted to capture this ship, but he also suspected a trap. He ordered what was subsequently identified as the NDL freighter *Chemnitz* to stop and his own submarine to dive. The German stopped. Back to the surface came *Poncelet*, her bow tubes menacing the enemy.

Both sides watched the other tensely. At any moment the Germans would see torpedo tracks surging towards them. At any moment, the Frenchmen would see flaps dropping and hidden guns opening fire. Neither happened. The Germans did as they were bade, most of them taking to one of their lifeboats. A boarding party paddled over to *Chemnitz* in *Poncelet*'s little skiff, which returned bearing the German master, his first officer and the chief engineer. Kapitän Knubel had ordered the seacocks to be opened, but the *equipage de prise* (two officers and thirteen men) closed them, and then ordered the German lifeboat back alongside. The crew clambered back up the jumping ladder, to be welcomed by the muzzles of French guns. Most were marched forward and imprisoned in their own forecastle, while the engineers were taken below and told to get the ship under way. They were supervised by some of the Frenchmen, while the rest of the prize crew did all the navigation and deckwork. *Poncelet* kept watch during the voyage to Casablanca in rough, damp weather which brought on a recurrence of Lieutenant de Vaisseau de Saussine's lumbago.

It was said at the time that *Chemnitz* was the first ship in history to be captured and brought home by a submarine. Certainly it was the first such exploit in World War II. The cargo was bound from South America to Hamburg via Las Palmas and consisted of cotton, lead ingots, copper, flour and parrots, but found its way to France instead. *Chemnitz* herself was taken into French service as *Saint Bertrand*, her new name being chosen in honour of her captor. *Poncelet*'s celebration was enhanced by bottles of Rhein wine liberated from *Chemnitz*'s pantry.

The honour of securing the largest prize taken on the high seas during World War II—some said the biggest-ever mid-ocean capture—went to the Royal Navy. She was the 13,615-ton *Cap Norte* built in 1922 for the Hamburg-Südamerika Linie. She already had a minor place in Nazi lore. In 1935, she had met her sister-ship *Antonio Delfino* at sea and taken over an Argentinian-born German for trial back in the Fatherland. It was part of that policy which sought to prove that all Germans were subject to NSDAP laws wherever they had been born. On 22 September 1939, *Cap Norte* sailed from Pernambuco (a Brazilian port also known as Recife), partly crewed by reservists returning for service in the Kriegsmarine. The liner was unable to obtain as much fuel as she needed and was forced to attempt the Iceland-Faeroes Channel on 9 October 1939.

Approaching on a nearly reciprocal line of advance was *HMS Belfast*, the Royal Navy's newest and biggest cruiser with a deep load displacement of 14,325 tons. At the beginning of the forenoon watch a faint haze cut visibility to seven miles, but overhead the sky was blue and so was the sea, with white horses being flecked up by a moderate southeast wind. At 11.04 am, just two minutes after despatching the Norwegian freighter *Tai Yin* to Kirkwall under armed guard, *Belfast*'s lookouts sighted a single-funnelled ship with substantial white upperworks. She appeared to be the Swedish liner *Ancona* and bore that name on her counter. The next boarding party was piped topside and within an hour *Belfast*'s 32-foot cutter was being manned and lowered. By now the weather had deteriorated. Grey clouds scudded across under a thickening overcast. Dense patches of mist brushed the rising sea, occasional foaming crests appearing in the rare bright intervals. The pull across to the liner was rough and uncomfortable, the boat rising and falling ten feet at a time.

A rope ladder had been hung over the side from the forward well-deck, but it had to be jumped for. A climb of 25 to 30 feet followed, the weight of slung Lee-Enfield rifles threatening to drag the Royal Marines and ratings from their precarious hold. At the top, their fingers were pinched against the bulwarks, but they swung themselves over to face—an empty expanse of deck. There was nobody in sight. Engine Room Artificer George Finch (one of *Belfast*'s divers and always ready to vary the monotony with non-routine jobs) was second over the side. He gathered his section—one leading stoker and three stokers—and headed them into a lavatory compartment in the superstructure. ERA Finch had already loaded his Webley & Scott .45-inch (11.4-mm) revolver. He now told his men to load their .303-inch (7.7-mm) rifles. The leading stoker and one of the stokers complied; the other two had to be shown how to do it. ERA Finch then took his little band out of the lavatory, through a couple more doors and into a throng of crew, stewardesses and passengers. There were 164 men and seven women on board. The ratings pushed their way through and found the entrance to the engine room. Far below, a circle of white faces stared up. The entire complement of engineers and greasers seemed to be ringing the foot of the ladder. Displaying greater confidence than they felt, the navalmen clambered down, the muzzles of the rifles snagging in rungs and machinery. At first the foreigners could speak no English and by various means indicated that they were Swedish, but ERA Finch pointed out the various cast instruction plates clearly marked in German which were positioned about the engine toom. The game was up and presently somebody stretched a tentative finger towards ERA Finch's revolver and said 'That is a big gun.'

Meanwhile up on the bridge, *Cap Norte*'s master was facing even bigger muzzles, *Belfast*'s twelve 6-inch (15.2-cm) guns. The only resistance he could offer was silent comment on the Royal Navy's hirsute appearance; he proffered the bearded boarding officer a razor. By 1.47 pm the prize was on her way to the Orkneys and the cutter had returned to *Belfast*, taking with her the boarding party's rations, which had been left aboard in the excitement. The two officers and twenty ratings would have to depend upon German provisions—but suppose these were poisoned or doped? So, for the next day and a half, the British navalmen existed on what they could take from the galley during the preparation of German meals. The Hamburg-Südamerika cooks provided their officers with mid-watch snacks of sandwiches and biscuits served on silver trays, plus silver coffee-pots. These were requisitioned by British personnel on duty after a couple of German mouthfuls had proved their nutritional value.

What the Royal Navy could not understand was whether the order to open the seacocks had actually been given or whether it had been delayed en route to the engine room. Certainly they found and threw overboard a number of 5-kg (11-pound) sledgehammers and cold steel chisels secreted ready for fracturing the condenser inlet pipes. What they did not know was that when he sighted *Belfast*, the German master had decided the sea was too rough to scuttle and abandon. It was therefore arranged that all should be quiet and co-operative until nearing a British port. Several greasers would then jump the Royal Navy stokers in the boiler room and start smashing gauges there. ERA Finch and the couple with him would rush straight in from the engine room to see what was happening and be locked in. By the time they had made their plight known to the British on deck, enough damage would have been done in the engine room to ensure that *Cap Norte* never entered harbour, although close enough to shore for everybody to take to the boats in safety.

However, this conspiracy reached British ears and steps were taken to prevent it without arousing German suspicions. In the engine room, all the Germans were gradually sent up except the watchkeeping engineer. ERA Finch was not only qualified to take charge of an engine room and supervise stokers in their work, he had also served in *HMS Cyclops*. This old depot ship had reciprocating engines and ERA Finch therefore felt quite at home in *Cap Norte*'s engine room, even though the liner had two shafts, plus low-pressure exhaust-steam turbines. It did mean that he had to do almost everything on his own, including checking the temperature of working machinery by the time-honoured method of putting his palm vertically between the web and the crosshead of the piston.

The Germans did not seem unduly worried by the thwarting of their sabotage. As one of them explained: 'Many U-boote; soon many bangs; no *Belfast*.' Only in the last hours did they lose hope of rescue. Several tried to alleviate their despondency in drink, but the German officers smashed the bottles and maintained discipline without the British intervening.

There were different problems at Kirkwell. A large party of shorebased reservist bluejackets stormed aboard. Armed to the teeth, they treated everybody —British as well as Germans—with brusque suspicion. After twenty-eight hours on their feet, *Belfast*'s prize crew were at last able to get their heads down in comfortable cabins, snuggling under warm wood pulp blankets. *Cap Norte* was no longer their responsibility, but twice they were woken and appealed to by German merchant seamen, complaining of souvenir hunters and of the painful and embarrassing way in which the stewardesses were being lowered into waiting boats at the end of a line. *Belfast* was still out so her personnel were ordered to report aboard *Royal Oak*, lying in Scapa Flow. For some reason they could not be accommodated in her immediately, so they were directed to the AMC *Voltaire* for the next couple of days. During that time *Royal Oak* was torpedoed and sunk with heavy loss of life.

It was accordingly decided that the empty *Cap Norte* should be anchored to block one of the entrances. There seemed to be some satisfaction in consigning former German vessels to ignominious fates, but they soon found more active employment as the Battle of the Atlantic progressed. *Cap Norte* became the appropriately named *Empire Trooper* and survived the war.

5 Northern Patrol and Southern Hunt

By the end of 1939, seventeen German ships had been sunk or captured by the Northern Patrol alone. There seemed to be something different about every interception. On 19 October *Biscaya*'s chief engineer asked permission to scuttle when the tanker was intercepted by the armed merchant cruiser *Scotstoun* in the Denmark Strait. The master refused, pointing out that even if the engine room were flooded she would probably stay afloat on the buoyancy of her empty tanks. The crew would be risking gunfire to no purpose; instead they refused to co-operate with the prize crew, who had to work the ship themselves.

Bianca's officers were quite cheerful about the seizure of their vessel, also in the Denmark Strait. They assured the prize crew from the AMC *Transylvania* that a U–boat was coming to the rescue. When this did not materialize, the Germans suggested that the British keep the ship, but allow them to lower a lifeboat so that they could make their way back to Germany in that.

Three of *Gloria*'s crew tried to do this on the last night before their ship (captured by the cruiser *Sheffield*) arrived in Kirkwall. Cutting themselves adrift in a northerly gale, they sailed towards Norway for nearly a week before being stopped by a patrolling trawler. The British report said, 'This fine attempt deserved better fortune' (ADM199/390: *Northern Patrol*).

So did *Poseidon*. She had escaped the cruiser *Ajax* off South America, only to be caught by *Scotstoun* in the Denmark Strait on 21 October. The weather was too rough for scuttling or boarding, so the AMC escorted her prize to the lee of Iceland. From here on the Germans refused to work their ship. A boarding party got her under way, but could not maintain steam and had to be taken in tow. The tow parted in gale-force snowstorms. *Scotstoun* took off the crew at daybreak on 27 October and then sank *Poseidon* with gunfire.

Scotstoun ran into a solid ice-floe on 10 November 1939, buckling a frame and starting plates. Twice a day, some 24 tons of water were pumped out of the forepeak. It was not serious enough to abandon patrol and on 18 November her lookouts sighted a Swedish steamer. Boarded the next day, she proved to be the German *Eilbek*, burning part of her cargo of wood pulp as fuel . *Mecklenburg*'s master wanted to go down with his ship and had to be forcibly rescued . *Parana* coming from Montevideo had the Russian name *Iama* painted on her sides. When this failed to deceive the cruiser *Newcastle*, she was scuttled and set on fire. Even so, the boarding party captured her and brought her into port. The German master was heard complaining that this had happened to him at the beginning of the previous war.

The cruiser *Colombo*'s report described the crew of the SS *Henning Oldendorff* as '29 enthusiastic Nazis' (ADM199/390: *Northern Patrol*). They fell to fisticuffs over whose dereliction of duty had led to the capture of the ship and her 5000 tons of iron pyrites. On the whole most crews were composed of a few keen Nazis, a few fervent anti-Nazis, and the majority indifferent to all politics. Some interrogators noted that a number of survivors from German ships 'talked freely and gave information which it is hoped would not be given by British merchant seamen' (ADM1/10658: *Report of Proceedings from HMS Despatch*). Involuntary loquacity, a symptom of shock quite understandable in peacetime, became a reprehensible lapse of security in wartime.

Delhi was one of the cruisers whose prize crew had had time to be prepared for their role. They boarded the frieghter *Rheingold* after a warning 6-inch (15.2-cm) round had been fired. The engine room party found that the condenser door bolts had been removed and then shored up. A quick jerk on a lanyard and the water would have been foaming into the ship. But no one had pulled the lanyard. Why bother, explained the master. He would get his ship back in six to nine months' time when Germany had won the war.

Berta Fisser filled with water so quickly after being abandoned, that the AMC *Chitral* decided to finish her off with gunfire. 6-inch (15.2-cm) shells merely set her on fire and next day the hulk drifted ashore on Iceland. The following afternoon (22 November), her sister-ship *Konsul Hendrik Fisser* was caught by the cruiser *Calypso*. The weather was too rough to launch boats either for boarding or abandoning. Under the cruiser's 6-inch (15.2-cm) guns, the German freighter made her way to a rendezvous area in the lee of the land, where three Northern Patrol trawlers effected a capture.

The oft-repeated comment that U-boats were coming to the rescue was no vain hope, although the outcome was not necessarily what the Germans expected. At 1 pm on 18 November, Lieutenant-Commander B. Moloney, RNR, left the AMC *California* to take an armed party on board what appeared to be a Dutch ship. She proved to be the German *Borkum*, with a cargo of wheat. The master and most of the crew were transferred to *California*, leaving two German seamen, nine engine room ratings and a cook on board the prize, which set off for Kirkwall. In spite of fine weather, speed gradually dropped from eight knots to two knots. Lieutenant-Commander Moloney found that the bilge pipe-lines were choked with grain, while the Germans in the engine room, though co-operative, were getting progressively drunk. A search of the ship revealed 240 bottles in sleeping berths and the dirty linen store. These were thrown overboard, the ratings sobered up, the pipes were unblocked, and speed came back to 7 knots. At 3.30 pm on 23 November, *Borkum* was between Orkney and Shetland, when a U-boat appeared two miles away. It signalled 'Stop Engines' and overhauled the freighter. Wearing British colours over German, *Borkum* was hit by twelve rounds. With his prize well ablaze and steam-pipes severed, Lieutenant-Commander Moloney ordered 'Abandon Ship'. Several Germans were killed and others injured, but the survivors of both nationalities got away in two boats. One was leaking and they lost touch, but they were all picked up by the trawlers *Kingston Beryl* and *Kingston Onyx*.

Other German vessels intercepted and scuttled were *Gonzenheim*, *Tenerife* and *Antiochia*. In addition, a total of 243 neutral merchantmen were sent into Kirkwall, while 674 ships of all types and nationalities were sighted by the Northern Patrol during the last four months of 1939. There were, of course, many which were not sighted. As the year wore on, there were fewer than six hours of daylight in Icelandic latitudes. There was no radar; interception depended upon visual lookout in gale-force sleet and spray, in snowstorms so thick that everything beyond the ship's rail was hidden behind a silent curtain of white, and on nights so dark that the heaving sea could not be seen, only sensed. For days and nights there was no chance of checking a dead-reckoning position by sun- or star-sight. When two patrolling warships sighted each other and compared positions, the very fact of their meeting meant that the gap on either side was that much greater, favouring the blockade runners and neutrals who did not wish to be stopped and examined. Even close to, a lookout stamping his feet for warmth, screwing up his aching eyes, or wiping his binocular lenses, might miss that single, decisive glimpse.

Little *Lahnek*, owned by Deutsche Dampfschifffahrts-Gesellschaft Hansa and just 1663 gross tons, had been in Vigo harbour from 29 August to 11 November 1939. Once at sea, Kapitän Meyer disguised his ship as the Soviet freighter *Dvina*. He did not have all the relevant charts for northern waters, but he made for and passed through the Denmark Strait, arriving in Hamburg on 12 December. In the blackest hours of one night, what was apparently a British escort appeared out of the darkness, missed *Lahnek* by 60 feet and was swallowed up in obscurity again. Twice, in daylight, Kapitän Meyer sighted AMCs, but they either accepted his disguise and decided not to investigate closely, or failed to see him at all.

However, it might have happened that the British warships might not have been able to come round on an intercepting course quickly enough, so that the far blur became invisible again. Their human crews were willing, but the original cruisers of the Northern Patrol were getting old. *Effingham*, the youngest, had been launched in 1921. They were well built, but they had been in seagoing service for twenty years. Their hulls, engines and equipment felt the strain of the continual pounding of the northern winter. Reports spoke of aerials carried away under the weight of ice, whalers stove in, paravanes swept overboard, torpedo tubes and gun mountings jammed and steering gear damaged. Most had been designed for North Sea work and had to leave station to fuel more often than more modern ships. Of them all, *Emerald* fared best. Thanks to her knuckles and trawler bow (a feature shared with some of the Cs and Ds), plus larger fuel reserves, she was able to keep the sea for longer periods and at a higher speed. Accordingly, the older cruisers were gradually withdrawn from the Northern Patrol and reallocated to calmer climes.

The AMCs stayed, from 20 December 1939 under the command of Vice-Admiral R.H.T. Raikes. It might have been expected that, being larger, they would do better in these conditions. In fact, their bulk made them highly susceptible to wind, while their peaceful decks, though strengthened, were not intended to carry the weight of 6-inch (15.2-cm) gun mountings in midwinter storms. They were not built as men o' war, a fact demonstrated when they did engage enemy warships. Improvised hoists were too slow bringing up ammunition from many decks below. Their guns were old, unwanted by fleet vessels. Fire control instruments were the simplest rangefinders and calculators, data often being transmitted by word of mouth. Damage control may have been adequate for marine hazards, but not for dealing with hostilely inflicted fire and flooding.

The AMCs presented substantial targets to most naval weapons. *Rawalpindi* was sunk in action with *Scharnhorst* and *Gneisenau* southeast of Iceland on 23 November 1939, a loss which occasioned the temporary withdrawal of AMCs from the Northern Patrol. Later in the war, in other areas, *Jervis Bay* and *Voltaire* were sunk and *Carnarvon Castle* and *Alcantara* severely damaged in similar surface ship engagements. And when aircraft and U-boats began their long-range depredations, they inflicted heavy casualties on the lonely AMCs and OBVs. The Northern Patrol, from 16 July 1940 under Rear-Admiral Spooner, was wound up as a separate command on 10 June 1941.

The difficulties of sighting and intercepting a blockade runner were immense, but even if carried out satisfactorily, it might not be concluded successfully. The same date that *Cap Norte* was being boarded, a Fairey Swordfish from the carrier *Ark Royal* was circling and challenging a tanker southwest of Cape Verde. The vessel replied that she was the American *Delmar*. On board *Ark Royal*, Vice-Admiral L.V. Wells and Captain A.J. Power considered the signal. The tanker might have been *Delmar*. The only way to make certain was to go and see, but *Ark Royal* was without destroyers to screen her from the U-boats that had been rumoured in the area. So the carrier continued on course for Freetown, where she would join a group hunting a pocket battleship. Admiral and captain were not to know that the stranger was also going to meet *Admiral Graf Spee*. She was the German auxiliary oiler *Altmark; Delmar* was in New Orleans.

Next day, the Swordfish sighted another vessel, a freighter. She was wearing the Greek flag, but did not respond to the signals flashed at her. A warning bomb was dropped ahead of her, but she redoubled her efforts to escape, her funnel emitting clouds of smoke. Again she could not be boarded and was given the benefit of the doubt.

On 18 October 1939 it was the Norwegian flag which received attention from the *Ark*'s biplanes. This time the crew abandoned ship without waiting to be challenged. One of the Swordfish had to fly low over the lifeboats, dropping a message assuring the merchant seamen that they had been recognized as neutral and could reboard their ship without danger.

The identification of merchant ships at sea, even in ideal visibility, was a recurrent problem throughout the war. The biggest shipping companies required publicity pictures of their multi-funnelled floating hotels and modern cargo liners for prewar publicity, but there was no way of easily distinguishing the huge number of three-island cargo ships. Admittedly German freighters had a traditionally upright look to them—there was something different about their bridge and funnel—but German shipbuilders delivered vessels to all buyers, while many had been acquired by Allied countries as war reparations after 1919. However, no lone ship could be approached without due caution; it could easily be a trap. Standing off and opening fire on a minor target wasted ammunition. Even the best gunners could miss sometimes and any delay favoured escape if night was coming on. Besides, it was much better to capture an enemy ship; much better to confiscate neutral contraband than destroy it. And no Royal Navy captain wanted to be the one who caused a diplomatic incident by deliberately shooting at neutral civilians just because they were a bit slow at understanding the English language and naval procedure. It was only by boarding, that a merchant ship's identity could be established during the early war years—and even that was not infallible. The captains of Royal Navy Q-ships posing as merchantmen reported that intercepting warships approached incautiously and accepted incorrect signals, while boarding officers were satisfied with false papers and a cursory glance around the decks, completely failing to learn anything about the true nature of the vessel.

Even if a merchant ship were identified as German it was becoming increasingly difficult to capture blockade runners as 1939 wore on. By now German masters, officers and men were accepting the reality of war at sea and had had time to prepare their ships for scuttling, equipment for destruction and weighted bags ready to throw sensitive documents overboard. Explosive charges were placed against bulkheads, their detonation being preceded by the use of flare pistols to ignite petrol poured over the cargo and superstructure. Such incendiarism made life very difficult for a salvage team trying to halt the scuttling process. Even the possibility of booby-traps might make potential captors hesitate and search long enough for the vessel to settle irrecoverably with only her seacocks open.

This sabotage was not always successful in the early months of the war. Few seagoing civilians were demolitions experts. They did not always have the best explosives or locate them properly or set the fuzes correctly, but enough German ships foundered in flames to make the British Admiralty consider some sort of counter measure.

It was on 23 November 1939, that the British Cabinet agreed to sanction the sort of instructions that were already being promulgated. In future, German merchant vessels should be ordered to stop and then cast loose their lifeboats—empty. A further signal would inform the crews that if they attempted to scuttle their ship, they would be left aboard her to drown or burn. If they co-operated in the peaceful transfer of their craft, they would be taken off and treated properly. However, Royal Navy captains were also instructed always to rescue survivors, whether in boats or still on board, although the Germans were not to know that.

One problem that remained was how to persuade the German crew to tell where they had placed demolition charges and when they were going to explode. There was no point in chasing after the lifeboats if the crew had already abandoned ship because she was already sinking. That was wasting time which could be better spent going alongside and dealing with fire and flooding straightaway. Sometimes the charges had not gone off and some of the crew were still on board. Then, Royal Navy opinion favoured locking the saboteurs in a vulnerable compartment until they agreed to talk. This was tried by both sides during the war without much success, the most famous incidents being the Italian and British attacks on the battleships *Valiant* and *Tirpitz*.

It is difficult to ascertain the effect of this policy. Usually the scuttling process had been set in motion and the crew preparing to abandon long before the intercepting warship was close enough to challenge the stranger. Nor is it clear how far the policy was implemented. Being forced to leave survivors—friend or foe—to their fate because of operational necessity was one thing. Deliberately destroying—even threatening to destroy—the victims' means of survival, ran counter to the Royal Navy's—to any seafarer's—traditions of humanity. On the other side, the men in a lifeboat frantically pulling away from a sinking ship, did not see a cruiser shooting at a possible disguised raider whose own guns would be revealed as soon as the panic-party had cleared the range; they saw only a vengeful Britisher shelling helpless survivors who had dared to thwart his lust for prize.

What the Royal Navy did not know was that German radio intelligence (Beobachtungsdienst) had already intercepted the earliest Admiralty signals about this matter. The German merchant marine was warned of the Royal

Navy's intentions on 24 October 1939. Six days later all mercantile masters and officers were informed that anyone who allowed his ship to be captured, would face a court of enquiry when the war was over. What is normal procedure in every navy, acquired sinister overtones when laid down by the Nazis. However, most captains were already doing what they could to scuttle their ships, even without veiled threats or promises of honour.

During all this time, the British Admiralty was receiving intelligence reports of darkened merchantmen loading in or sailing from neutral ports. The information was of varied reliability, from naval attachés, black marketeers, gossiping sailors, or from one of His Majesty's submarines lying submerged just outside the three-mile limit. The arrival of rumour or report caused cruisers to steam many days on false alarms.

Meanwhile in Berlin, SKL was making its own dispositions. The *panzerschiff Admiral Graf Spee* had been operating in the southern tropics since the beginning of the war. Among other things, she needed carbon dioxide for the magazine refrigerating machinery which kept her ammunition cool and stable. The 4372-ton tanker *Emmy Friedrich* lying at Tampico in Mexico included carbonic acid in her cargo. She was ordered to sail on 20 October 1939 and rendezvous.

On the map, the West Indies look like a barrier across the Caribbean stretching from North to South America. It is a barrier with many gaps. The British and French navies did not have enough warships to watch every channel. There was just a chance that once *Emmy Friedrich* had passed into the broad Caribbean, the searchers would not be able to guess which exits she would choose. *Emmy Friedrich* never had that chance. The great Gulf of Mexico is separated from the Caribbean proper by the 120-mile Yucatan Channel. There lay the British cruiser *Orion* and the Canadian destroyer *Saguenay*. They sighted the tanker in the distance and turned her back into the Gulf of Mexico. Their reports guided another cruiser, *Caradoc*, on an intercepting course. *Emmy Friedrich* scuttled herself on 23 October.

The threat posed by the Atlantic and Indian Ocean forays of the *panzerschiffe Deutschland* and *Admiral Graf Spee* caused considerable Allied activity in areas where British and French squadrons were not usually seen in force. Just as policemen investigating homicide uncover a host of lesser offences, so these concentrated naval searches coincidentally discovered a number of German merchantmen hoping to get through to European waters in the North Atlantic winter.

First to be swept up was *Hallé*, a freighter of 5889 tons. She was encountered by the French cruiser *Duguay-Trouin* west of Dakar on 16 October. She scuttled herself. Another French cruiser, *Dupleix*, backed up the French destroyers *Le Fantasque* and *Le Terrible* when they sighted the 4627-ton *Santa Fé*. The freighter's course had taken her too close to the Force de Raide covering an otherwise unescorted convoy from Kingston in Jamaica. *Santa Fé* scuttled herself on 25 October.

Next to go was *Uhenfels*, a Hansa freighter of 7603 tons. She had spent the early weeks of the war at Lourenço Marques in Portuguese Mozambique. She had a cargo of copra, cotton and opium and had broken out on 13 October. The sixty-one men on board were on short rations when, off Freetown on 5 November, a single-engined biplane appeared, a Swordfish from *Ark Royal*. Then three warships hove in sight. *Uhenfels* was fast—14 knots—but she could not outrun these pursuers. Kapitän Schuldt ordered most of his crew into the lifeboats while he and the remainder opened the seacocks. The engine room did not flood quickly enough. A party from the destroyer rushed aboard. Pumps were started and *Uhenfels* towed into Freetown. The consignment of opium alone was valued at a quarter of a million pounds; its medical worth was inestimable.

When war was declared, another Hansa ship, *Trifels*, had been coming home from India. Faced with the mutiny of fifty-seven Indian seamen and greasers who did not want to go to Germany, Kapitän Ihlefeld called at Lourenço Marques and exchanged them for Germans from other ships, plus overseas residents who wanted to get home. He reached the Azores but it was not until 12 November that he judged it safe for *Trifels* to continue her voyage. By then she had been prepared for scuttling. When, two days later, the French AMC *Koutoubia* intercepted her, 1000 litres (220 gallons) of high-octane petrol stowed in No. 4 Hold were ignited and the crew abandoned ship. To their disappointment there was no mighty conflagration. Instead the fire went out of its own accord and *Trifels* was taken as prize to Casablanca.

Lobito in Portuguese Angola shielded *Adolph Woermann* until 16 November. She was posing as the Portuguese liner *Nyassa* for the South American leg of her journey home when, four days out, she fell in with the Shaw Savill cargo liner *Waimarama*. Her master knew the real *Nyassa* and where she was. He suspected something about the other vessel's appearance and began shadowing her at a suitable distance. That night the two unarmed merchantmen manoeuvred in their own private war as the 8577-ton *Adolph Woermann* came out of the darkness apparently trying to ram the 12,843-ton *Waimarama*. She then sheered off and was lost to sight.

Meanwhile Force K, consisting of the battlecruiser *Renown* and the carrier *Ark Royal*, was on its way. The two capital ships were usually accompanied by four H-class destroyers and by one or more of the locally based cruisers. One destroyer acted as plane-guard astern of the carrier, ready to recover aircrew in the event of a flight-deck accident. The other three destroyers provided an anti-submarine screen unless U-boats were not anticipated. Then Force K opened out into a broad line abreast, so that the maximum area of search swathed across the ocean; a further crescent ahead and on either side was covered by the *Ark*'s Swordfish. Having reached the limits of their patrol zone, the Force turned and swept back along an adjacent rectangle. The monotony was occasionally broken by fuelling at Freetown, by sighting and investigating some lone merchantman, or by Admiralty orders to intercept a reported enemy. In this case it was *Waimarama*'s signal about the suspicious *Nyassa*. The cruiser *Neptune* was nearest and she steered in that direction, while that night Force K encountered a dark shape; the New Zealand cargo liner *Opawa* came close to receiving a salvo of friendly shells. The real *Adolph Woermann* was intercepted by *Neptune* near Ascension Island on 22 November. The fleeing liner stopped and scuttled herself. The cruiser rescued 135 men, twenty-five women and two children.

Watussi and *Windhuk* were two of the finest liners of the Woermann Linie. They were both turbine-driven, both twin-funnelled. *Windhuk* was the larger at 16,662 gross tons. Completed in 1937, her two propellers gave her speed of 18 knots. She was at Lobito in Angola in November 1939, separated by the African continent from her 9521-ton sister at the port of Mozambique. Both were ordered to sail for South America, *Watussi* departing on 22/23 November. She was an older ship and could do only 13.5 knots down through the Mozambique Channel and round the coast of South Africa.

Only a week before *Watussi*'s departure, *Admiral Graf Spee* had advertised her presence in the Indian Ocean. The British hunting groups concentrated off the Cape of Good Hope, their line of search straddling the pocket battleship's route back into the South Atlantic. But their quarry had already passed that way, 300-400 miles offshore. Not so grey-painted *Watussi*, just 90 miles south of Cape Agulhas and proceeding west into the safe expanse of the South Atlantic.

At 10.16 am on 2 December, her crew sighted a Junkers Ju86 airliner, but they could derive no comfort from its German appearance or the sound of its Junkers Jumo engines. This plane had once belonged to South African Airways. Now armed, it was part of No. 15 Bomber Reconnaissance Squadron, South African Air Force. The squadron's three aircraft, each with a range of 980 miles, took turns to patrol as far as 140 miles to the south. Captain Boshoff had found *Watussi*.

The Ju86 circled, broadcasting the enemy's position, course and speed. Then it came in at low-level, the mid-upper gunner firing across the liner's bows. A bomb close alongside persuaded the German master to steer northwards, but he resumed his original course as soon as shortage of fuel forced the aircraft to make for home. A second Ju86 arrived at 1 pm, again making *Watussi* head north after Kapitän Stäner had replied to the aircraft's signals with 'Ship stops old man.' Meanwhile the two other aircraft were getting ready for take-off as soon as they had been fuelled. The carrier *Ark Royal* made sure that at least two Swordfish maintained a standing patrol over the liner. *Renown* and the cruiser *Sussex* were on their way.

At 3.25 pm *Watussi* was but 60 miles from the South African coast when she was seen to stop and begin lowering her boats. The Germans were obviously going to scuttle and could not be dissuaded even when warned by South African machine-guns and a Fleet Air Arm smoke float. Sunlight sparkled on the water as *Watussi*'s after hatch belched smoke. She was soon ablaze from stem to stern, settling as water poured in through the opened seacocks. The survivors, who included women (one due for confinement at any time) and children, were recovered from lifeboats by *Sussex*. The blazing derelict was now listing so that her starboard rail was under water. Captain Power of *Ark Royal* had once commanded *HMS Excellent*, the Royal Navy's gunnery school. Aircraft carrier gunners rarely have the chance to display their skills against surface targets. They seized their opportunity, but after several 4.5-inch (11.4-cm) shells had been despatched, *Renown* intervened, signalling 'Now let a gunnery ship have a go' (Poolman, *Ark Royal*). Using the two 15-inch (38.1-cm) guns in one turret only, the battlecruiser sank *Watussi*.

The temporary diversion of British forces away from the central South Atlantic had ended *Watussi*'s career, but proved beneficial for *Windhuk*. She reached Santos in Brazil on 7 December.

Not so fortunate was the Deutsche Afrika Linie (DAL) *Ussukuma*. She had arrived at Bahia Blanca in Argentina from Lourenço Marques on 13 October. She had to fuel before returning to Germany and the nearest place with sufficient stocks was Montevideo, 600 miles along her route. The 7834-ton liner sailed on 4 December, but next day her distinctive passenger decks were sighted by the cruiser *Ajax* patrolling off the River Plate. *Ussukuma*'s master tried to escape in the gathering dusk and then decided to scuttle. A boarding party got away promptly, but returned when night closed in. Next morning the German liner had disappeared.

In the Pacific, a prize crew from the cruiser *Despatch* was able to capture the 4930-ton freighter *Düsseldorf* off Punta Caldera in Chile on 5 December. The chief engineer had tried to destroy the main circulator inlet with a bomb, but it had not gone off properly. However, the ship was not in a fit condition for a long voyage, so Commodore Allan Poland took *Despatch* into Antofagasta. Thanks to the British consul's good relations with the Chilean authorities, permission was granted for *Düsseldorf* to enter harbour for repairs and fuel. This done, the freighter departed under armed guard, minus one crew-member who had escaped ashore. The ship's stewardess also asked to remain in Chile, but she had to 'proceed in prize' to Jamaica with her compatriots. Although he could not be blamed for the failure of his scuttling attempt, the German master was worried about what would happen to him after the war. British assurances that Germany would then be under new management were no comfort.

On 9 December the German tanker *Nordmeer* sailed from Curaçao, giving the French submarine *Ouessant* the slip amongst the passages of the Antilles. She was bound for Vigo with a cargo of oil.

That same day, the cruiser *Shropshire* was on anti-raider patrol on the Cape Town-St Helena route when lookouts sighted *Adolf Leonhardt*. The Germans scuttled their ship and the Allies lost another 2990 tons of valuable shipping.

She was the last German merchantman to be caught up in the search for *Admiral Graf Spee* who was brought to battle four days later. Throughout the whole campaign, lonely *Erlangen* had been making her stealthy way towards some safe haven. She had left Carnley Harbour on 6 October. Sometimes under makeshift sail and with her crew suffering from malnutrition, she had at last reached Puerto Monti in southern Chile on 12 November.

6 Neutral Attitudes

The European goal of all these blockade runners, even if they paused at an intermediate neutral port, was the Indreled, a passage along the Norwegian coast, sheltered from the open sea by a multitude of islands. On the landward side, intricate fjords penetrated the mountains, affording further protection from ocean storms and hostile observation. The route was, of course, within Norway's three-mile limit, but there was no legal objection to its use by bona fide merchantmen of any nationality. The Norwegian auxiliaries were allowed to search such vessels to verify this fact. They were not permitted to search a foreign warship, but then, warships were not supposed to be there. There were problems regarding merchantmen serving as unarmed naval authorities (concealed armament often counted as 'unarmed'). They could not be searched because they were warships, nor could they be denied passage, because they were merchant ships engaged in commercial tasks, although paid by the government. In such cases the vessel was formally visited, cursory observation establishing that she was unarmed. She was then escorted by the Royal Norwegian Navy to ensure that she behaved herself. If it were learned that this merchantman was using territorial waters for some belligerent purpose (such as the transport of prisoners of war), the Norwegian government could give her master three alternatives. He must either cease his belligerent activity (ie release the prisoners), or allow his ship and crew to be interned, or leave territorial waters. If he did none of these things, other powers could claim that because the enemy had infringed international law, they too could enter territorial waters, either to apprehend that particular offender, or to take suitable measures to prevent such a situation recurring.

This was the significance of the *City of Flint* case in 1939. On 9 October, the *panzerschiff Deutschland* stopped this American freighter southeast of Newfoundland. It was decided that though neutral, she was carrying 5000 tons of conditional contraband to Great Britain and could therefore be seized under the rules of prize warfare. With an armed German party on board, plus prisoners from the British *Stonegate*, *City of Flint* was disguised as the Danish *Elf* and despatched to Germany, calling at Tromso en route and claiming to be a bona fide member of the German mercantile marine. Now this was against the rules, which specified that prizes must be taken directly to one of the captor's ports. If an intermediate call were made—except in an emergency—then the ship must be handed back to her original crew and owners. Some of the armed guard's weapons had been thrown overboard, but the Norwegians also insisted that the British prisoners be released, which was done. Because she had no charts for the southward passage, *City of Flint* headed northwards, reaching Murmansk, now wearing the Kriegsmarine ensign. After staying several days, *City of Flint* once more entered Norwegian territorial waters, but this time her reception was different. Quite apart from the legal implications of the case, the Norwegians were not feeling particularly sympathetic towards the German cause, since one of their merchant ships, *Lorentz W. Hansen*, had been sunk by *Deutschland*. After various discussions at Tromso, *City of Flint* was hemmed in by two Norwegian warships on 3 November. The Germans surrendered and were interned. *City of Flint* was returned to her master, later proceeding to Narvik and then back to America.

During this incident, British warships stood guard near Stadlandet, where *City of Flint* would have been forced out to sea, but even here German ships returning from Murmansk took care to keep within or very close to the three-mile limit as they rounded the headland. Only on the final run across the Skagerrak and Heligoland Bight were German ships well away from neutral territorial waters; and even here there were rules to be observed. It was here while Lieutenant-Commander Bickford was giving the liner *Bremen* repeated fair warning on 12 December 1939, that a Dornier Do18 flying boat appeared and forced the submarine *Salmon* to dive. *Bremen* swept on to the safety of Columbuskaje at Bremerhaven and a fiery end at the hands of a disgruntled arsonist.

Even in their observation, international laws governing the war at sea could be subject to interpretation by belligerents who could plead operational necessity or special circumstances, by neutrals who feared or favoured one side more than the other. The most powerful neutral was the United States. The ruthless interruption of her overseas trade and interference in New World affairs had been the most important reasons for American entry into World War I. President Roosevelt was determined to prevent a repetition of such incidents in the western hemisphere. On 2 October 1939, at a conference in Panama, the various republics of the Americas, not only declared their intention of keeping out of the European conflict, but warned the belligerents against using the New World as a battleground. The western Atlantic from New England to Tierra del Fuego up to a distance of 600 miles from the coast was designated the Pan-

American Neutrality Zone. Parts of this area were already being patrolled by units from the US Navy's Atlantic Squadron.

At first it had been only a token presence, merely watching the warships and merchantmen of both sides without performing any unneutral act. However, agreements meant that British and French warships were not to exercise contraband control within this area, so neutral (principally American) merchant-men were free from harassment here. Allied merchant ships were content to mind their own business, but German vessels were something different. They might be converted as raiders or might fuel U-boats preying upon American shipping without declaration of war. So that they could be immediately eliminated if they did initiate any hostile action, they would have to be shadowed by American units the instant they left port. Relieving forces would have to be directed to the scene as quickly as possible—and that meant making signals in plain language. The US Navy was already demonstrating that partiality which was later embodied in a policy of all aid to Britain short of war.

On 13 and 14 December, two German ships sailed from Vera Cruz in Mexico. One was the freighter *Arauca*. The other, the first to leave, was the NDL liner *Columbus*. She grossed 32,581 tons and was the third largest vessel in the German merchant navy. At the beginning of the war, *Columbus* had been on a Caribbean cruise. Her American passengers were disembarked at Havana, before she reached Vera Cruz on 4 September. Here the consul gave Kapitän Dähne his orders to sail in the darkest period of the North Atlantic winter. It would be risky, but a successful escape would have considerable propaganda value. For a fortnight the crew of 557 was exercised in scuttling and abandoning ship.

The liner kept her speed down to 16-18 knots to conserve fuel for the long voyage around Iceland to Norway. One possible route was through the Yucatan Channel, but this was guarded by the Australian cruiser *Perth* watched in turn by the American cruiser *Vincennes* and two destroyers.

Columbus was not going that way, but as she left the Gulf of Campeche, two American destroyers hove in sight. They kept company, apparently a protective escort against British aggression. Across the wide Gulf of Mexico, through the Straits of Florida and out into the Atlantic went the liner and her shadows, the original pair being relieved by others of the same command until the cruiser *Tuscaloosa* took over. All the time the American ships had been broadcasting their own positions in plain language—as anybody is entitled to do if they so wish. It could not be helped if the Royal Navy happened to overhear those reports, just happened to guess what was happening, and made preparations to receive a German ship at the very moment she left the Pan-American Neutrality Zone. HMS *Hyperion*, her ship's company unhappy with the cold of Nova Scotia after the warmth of West Africa and the West Indies, was ordered to proceed from Halifax to Bermuda with all despatch. After a hurried conference, the destroyer sailed again, making for an area about 300 miles off Cape Hatteras.

Columbus was sighted on the port bow early in the Afternoon Watch of 19 December. Action Stations was sounded, a blank round fired and then a shot off the liner's bows emphasized the flag signal that had been hoisted for her to heave-to. *Hyperion*'s Captain St John Nicholson had trained two boarding parties for just such an opportunity as this. It had included revolver practice, which had proved somewhat disappointing for proficient rifle marksmen. A target was erected on the starboard guard rail and the revolvers fired from the port side of the ship. The distance was no more than 33 feet, but the roll of the ship made it difficult even to hit the target, let alone group the shots. Still, when boarding, the revolvers would probably have been used at a much closer range than ten yards. The prospective boarders never found out . . .

Within minutes, smoke was coming from the liner's decks and her lifeboats were being lowered, the crew abandoning ship in an orderly manner. Meanwhile a warship's superstructure had appeared over the horizon. It was not a pocket battleship come to the rescue, but *Tuscaloosa*, who was now addressed by Captain Nicholson. There seemed to be hundreds of Germans in the lifeboats rising and falling in the gentle swell, far too many able-bodied enemies for the destroyer's complement of 145 to overwhelm or accommodate. Accordingly *Tuscaloosa* agreed to recover the Germans—two of whom lost their lives—and land them in the United States. The American captain was also asked not to disclose *H97*, the pendant number painted on *Hyperion*'s bow. Once the cruiser had departed, the British destroyer circled the blazing derelict, which was sending up a great pall of smoke and listing slightly to port. The ship's company secured from Action Stations and went to Cruising Stations. During the night the liner's funnels collapsed and fell into the sea, her funeral pyre lighting up the ocean. It was a sad sight for anyone who loved ships, although the Royal Navy understood the motives behind such destruction. British newspapers and films, however, tended to give the impression that there was something cowardly or shameful about scuttling such beautiful vessels.

Columbus sank early in the Morning Watch of 20 December. That forenoon *Hyperion* went alongside the German lifeboats which had been left drifting after the recovery of their occupants. They were well provisioned with cases of meat, dried fruit and wine, items of greater service to *Hyperion*'s ship's company than to seagulls or fish. Six of the lifeboats were taken on a single long tow as they might find favour with the Sea Scouts in Bermuda, but the weather deteriorated, nearing hurricane force within a few hours. One by one the six boats were lost, to the accompaniment of speculation that if this blow had come earlier, it might have made the German master decide not to scuttle and abandon in such conditions. *Hyperion* would then have had the honour of capturing the largest prize at sea. There was some consolation in entering Bermuda on Christmas Day.

The crew of *Columbus* were not out of the war yet. Many of them were reservists and technicians, determined to help their country and avenge the loss of their ship. They, and other German nationals, intended to set out across the United States and then travel to Honolulu, where they would board a Japanese liner for Yokohama. A short sea journey to Korea, and they could catch a Trans-Siberian train back to Germany. Their progress was financed by American firms with German interests and subsidiaries, such as Standard Oil, and was watched by British Intelligence, but on 19 December 1939, attention was being concentrated on *Arauca*. The freighter was sighted by three US Navy aircraft near Miami. Their reports brought the British cruiser *Orion* to the scene, but her quarry stayed in territorial waters and entered Port Everglades.

Although co-operative in some matters, the United States government nevertheless objected to high-handed British action. On 4 November 1939, the American Neutrality Law had forbidden private citizens of the United States, their ships and aircraft to enter certain clearly defined war zones. These varied as hostilities spread, but the principal one comprised the Atlantic coast of France, the British Isles, the North Sea and the Baltic. The freighter *Mormacsun*, on passage from North America to Bergen, was routed outside this hazardous area—until 3 January 1940. On that date she was stopped by the Northern Patrol and taken to the Kirkwall examination centre—inside the forbidden war zone. The resulting complaint occasioned Winston Churchill's order that no more American ships should be stopped at sea or brought into prohibited areas.

There is no doubt that it was dangerous. The Norwegian *Belpamela* and the Swedish *Lagaholm* were both attacked by a U-boat while en route to Kirkwall on the night of 1/2 March 1940, the latter being sunk. There were other hazards, too. Approaching land is always perilous and no captain likes going in and out of harbour unnecessarily. The Norwegian freighters *Mim* and *Hansi* ran aground and were wrecked while obeying British commands to report at Kirkwall. The Norwegian War Insurance Club informed masters that their cover would lapse or their premiums be increased if they went south of Shetland. A combined protest document-cum-compensation claim was issued for masters to hand to British boarding officers. They were instructed by their authorities to accept this note without comment on receipt. The armed guard also had to be prepared to work the ship without co-operation from the neutral crew.

In the Far East there were other diplomatic exchanges. On 21 January 1940, twenty-one former members of German merchant ship crews (including *Columbus*) were taken off the Japanese liner *Asama Maru* by the cruiser *Liverpool*. It was a perfectly legal interception of a neutral ship, but the angry Japanese said that the Emperor had been personally insulted because the sacred snow-covered cap of Fujiyama was in sight a hundred miles away. At the same time, the Japanese were annoyed with the Germans because of the Nazi-Soviet Non-Aggression Pact. Accordingly the Japanese promised that in future they would not accept German reservists, technicians or civilians eligible for military service aboard their ships, although other civilians could travel as passengers.

In return the Australian AMC *Kanimbla* took nine bona fide noncombatant merchant seamen to Yokohama on 29 February 1940 so that they could continue their interrupted journey. Their German passengers were a source of great interest to the Australians. They noted that the most popular dishes were cold meat and salad, hot corned beef, fried eggs and sauté potatoes. They were big coffee drinkers—with milk—but could not stand pickles and sauces. The Admiralty was informed that 'The German officers and men made great inroads into scones and jam without butter. One wardroom fork is missing, probably taken as a souvenir' (ADM199/969: *Reports of Proceedings of HM Ships on South Atlantic Station*).

The British government still maintained its belligerent right to intercept contraband to and from Germany via Vladivostock, but without interfering with Japanese ships. Royal Navy penetration of the Sea of Japan was a hypothetical rather than a practical consideration, but something could be done to the east of Japan, and *Kanimbla* was assigned to this area. It was learned that a neutral Russian merchantman was coming from the United States with a cargo of copper. There were drills and firing practices for the AMC's boarding party which consisted of three officers and fourteen men, most of whom had Merchant Navy experience.

Vladimir Mayakovsky was stopped on 15 March 1940, but it was so rough that it was not until the next day that the boarding party could go over. They took with them twenty pistols and twenty-five rounds per man, rations for fourteen days, signalling equipment, a medicine chest and a flit gun for spraying anti-flea kerosene. The Russian vessel had to be fuelled and watered during the succeeding voyage, while running repairs also had to be carried out. It was not until 26 March that *Kanimbla* neared Hong Kong and handed her charge over to the French cruiser *Lamotte-Picquet*.

There was now less cause for neutral merchant ships to be stopped on the high seas. As the war progressed, there was much greater control of contraband at source. Navicerts were being issued by British representatives in foreign countries after receiving—and checking—guarantees of the cargo's destination before the neutral ship left port. The document of approval was attached to the ship's papers, its number being transmitted by telegram to the Contraband Committee in London, ready for the merchantman's arrival at examination centre or patrol line.

There was still a possibility that neutral countries might re-export material which the Contraband Committee had released for their use only. So the Ministry of Economic Warfare began assessing the resources and reserves, and estimating the future requirements, of all neutrals. The British government then rationed the number of ships allowed through the blockade to any one neutral. Surplus cargo was turned back or diverted—with proper payment—to British use, lest it be resold to Germany or stockpiled ready for future hostilities against the Allies.

1. Her paint scarred by Atlantic seas, *HMS Berwick* returns to Bermuda after another fruitless patrol in November 1939. She survived the war and when she was broken up two seats were made from the wood of her quarterdeck. They can be seen in the Herb Garden of the Red House Museum at Christchurch in Dorset.

2. A boarding party going away from *HMS Hilary* in the central Atlantic in 1941. Although wearing steel helmets and lifejackets, the ratings' rifles are stowed in the bottom of the boat. They will only be issued if resistance is encountered.

3. How not to do it – a Town-class cruiser on the Northern Patrol in 1939. On this occasion the Royal Navy suffered only a loss of dignity, but the incident illustrates the hazards of contraband control in the open sea.

4. 51,731 gross tons at 28 knots – *Bremen*, Germany's biggest merchant ship, gives a prewar demonstration of the speed which enabled her to escape the Royal Navy in 1939.

5. The Norddeutscher Lloyd liner *Columbus* was the largest Axis merchantman to be intercepted and scuttled on the high seas in World War II. Measuring 32,581 gross tons, she is seen here leaving Southampton in happier days.

6. With the Swedish name *Ancona* painted on her stern, the Hamburg-Südamerika *Cap Norte* was stopped southeast of Iceland on 9 October 1939. At 13,615 gross tons, she was the biggest ship captured on the high seas.

7. *Cap Norte* was intercepted by the cruiser *Belfast*, seen here at anchor in 1939. *HMS Belfast* is still afloat, now serving as a naval museum in the Pool of London.

8. The freighter *Chemnitz*, seen passing the new cruiser *Admiral Hipper*, was captured by the French submarine *Poncelet* in September 1939.

9. A prewar portrait of *Biscaya*, captured by the armed merchant cruiser *Scotstoun* in the Denmark Strait in October 1939. She was empty at the time, but such vessels could be used for the transport of both fuel and edible oils, with appropriate tank-cleaning in between.

10. Cormorants salute the German liner *Adolph Woermann* as she leaves Cape Town on a peacetime voyage. Her eventual interception came about after she had been shadowed by a British merchantman in the South Atlantic.

11. *Watussi* passes the destroyer *Escort* at the Silver Jubilee Spithead Review of 1935. On 2 December 1939 the German liner was scuttled off South Africa, being finished off by the guns of the battlecruiser *Renown* – seen here in the left background.

12. *Ussukuma* was the third German merchant ship to be intercepted by the cruiser *Ajax* in 1939.

13. The Deutsche Afrika Linie *Wangoni* not only evaded the Northern Patrol, but later escaped the British submarine *Triton* which intercepted her on 28 February 1940.

14. Pretending to be a neutral American, the German *Uruguay* is set on fire in the Denmark Strait on 6 March 1940.

15. Note the coat of arms of her namesake-city just above *Hannover*'s anchor. A salvage team from the cruiser *Dunedin* prevented her loss after she had been scuttled in the West Indies. She eventually became the escort carrier *Audacity*.

16. The armed merchant cruiser *Maloja* was converted from a P&O liner. She is seen here on the Clyde in 1940. She later became a troopship and survived the war.

17. The Norwegian freighter *Tropic Sea* in German hands in the South Pacific in June 1940.

There was also pre-emptive purchasing, whereby British representatives bought up all the stocks of some particular product of greater importance to the German than to the Allied economy. It was once suggested that such consignments could simply be dumped at sea, but invariably a use was found for them. The general public had no knowledge of these activities and often marvelled at the sudden quantities of unfamiliar foodstuffs in the shops.

None of these procedures could be organized overnight. Some took many years to establish. Sometimes exceptions were made for friendly neutrals or for those who might be coaxed into friendship. A black marketeer might still be allowed to handle his particular goods because he was a reliable source of information about something else. Secret agents found out which companies were likely to participate in the preparation of secret fuelling stations for U-boats and—depending on the agent's persuasion—steps taken to foil or encourage them. There were whispered assignations, drinks in bars, car accidents, suitcases of money diverted en route, clandestine transmitters tapping out codewords. Of course the other side was just as active, bribing, threatening, promising the rewards or punishments that would be meted out after the war. Faced with so many bewildering choices, so many ways of giving offence, few neutrals felt confident enough to declare their open support for one side or the other, even when they might have been expected to have a preference. Certainly those within a powerful belligerent's sphere of influence were anxious not to provoke military or economic aggression. In any case, why should a trade which had been perfectly proper and profitable a few months previously, be stopped just because a third party had quarrelled with the customer?

So the iron-ore shipments from northern Sweden continued on their way to Germany. In the winter of 1939/40, the Gulf of Bothnia was frozen over, preventing their shipment from Lulea. Instead, trainloads of ore rumbled through the mountains to the Norwegian ice-free port of Narvik, whence they could be despatched southwards via the Indreled. The stream of vessels was augmented by successful blockade runners, both mercantile and auxiliary.

7 Troubled Waters

The freighter *Konsul Horn* cleared Aruba in the Dutch West Indies on 7 January 1940. French and British warships patrolling off the island did not see her go. Nor could the French submarine *Agosta* catch her as she passed through the channels of the Lesser Antilles. Her Soviet disguise fooled both US Navy aircraft and the British cruiser *Enterprise*. Then *Konsul Horn* was alone, using the dark storms of the North Atlantic to cloak her from the watchers of the Northern Patrol.

Maritime hazards do not lose their perils just because they are being exploited for warlike purposes. Ahead of *Konsul Horn* was *Bahia Blanca*, coming from St Vincent. Assuming that British warships would leave a respectful distance between themselves and the Greenland ice, her master took her in as close as he could—too close. *Bahia Blanca* struck a berg and stuck fast for a time. When she did get free, water was pouring in and she foundered on 10 January. An SOS had been sent out and her crew were rescued by an Icelandic trawler.

Konsul Horn was more fortunate, reaching Norwegian waters on 6 February 1940. She delivered some of her cargo of sugar, having burnt the rest in her coal-fired boilers to keep going.

Behind *Konsul Horn* came a series of independents from South America and a half-dozen vessels from Vigo. When several ships sailed at or about the same time, they dispersed in the hope that the successful interception of one would serve as diversions covering the others. During their time in Vigo, the German crews were partly paid by the local consul, the balance being sent to their dependents in Germany, or held against their return home. The consul also passed on the sailing orders, although he could not provide any navigational or routeing advice. The Kriegsmarine did nothing to help, much to the disgust of the mercantile masters. The British Admiralty was warned of their imminent departure and a special force was concentrated in Western Approaches Command to deal with them as soon as they sailed, which they did on the night of 10/11 February.

Rostock had only just left neutral waters when she was stopped and seized by the French sloop *Elan*. Because her attention was focussed on *Rostock* the sloop was unable to pursue another two ships briefly illuminatd by searchlight. These were *Wahehe* and *Morea*. The former was later ignored by a British destroyer and French aircraft, while *Morea* claimed to be Danish when sighted by a destroyer 500 miles out in the Atlantic at 9.48 am on 12 February. *Hasty* came round in a wide circle to make sure it was not a U-boat trap and then lowered her whaler. A nasty sea was running, but *Morea*'s master immediately ordered his ship to be scuttled and abandoned. As soon as he saw what was happening, Lieutenant-Commander Tyrwhitt ordered the destroyer's .5-inch (12.7-mm) machine-guns to fire across the lifeboat, over the merchantmen's forecastle and then into her bridge. The Germans in the boat were told that they would not be picked up and were driven back to their ship, splashed by water thrown up by Lewis gun fire from *Hasty*. Meanwhile, Lieutenant Hart, the boarding officer, had prevented the other lifeboat from being lowered by discharging his revolver into its underside.

The bluejackets scrambled up. A signalman dashed to the wireless office, stopped the operator in the middle of tapping out a message, and temporarily put the set out of action. Down in the engine room, water was fountaining from the auxiliary circulator, fire and bilge pump sea inlet. The cover and 8-inch valve had been removed, but Lieutenant Williams and his section stuffed the hole with mattresses, put a steel plate on top and held it down with vertical wooden shores and wedges. The flow was checked and then stopped. One and a half hours later, the water had been pumped out and *Morea* was on her way. The boarding party obtained the goodwill of the Germans. They joined a Channel convoy and anchored in Falmouth Roads five days later.

For the time being, the other four Vigo ships had got away, but *Wakama* was not so lucky. She sailed from Rio de Janeiro on 11/12 February. Only hours later she was being scuttled off Cabo Frio as *Dorsetshire* came in sight, summoned by the cruiser's Walrus aircraft.

For a while in February 1940, the eyes of the world were turned on Norwegian waters as *Admiral Graf Spee*'s oiler *Altmark* made her homeward way through the Indreled. The Royal Navy maintained that she was a prison ship violating territorial waters, but her status as an auxiliary meant that she had been visited, not searched, by Norwegian officers. The Admiralty decided that the circumstances justified the British penetration of neutrality. The result was the release of 299 captives and the conviction amongst naval authorities on both sides that something definite must be done to safeguard their own and prevent the enemy's use of the Indreled.

Meanwhile the Vigo ships were making their several ways towards the area of the Northern Patrol. *Wahehe*, a DAL ship of 4709 tons, had sheltered in Vigo after sailing from Hamburg with a prewar export cargo of cement, mouth organs, dried fish, flour, motor cars, pigs' trotters, chemicals, umbrellas, rice, liquor, trousers, gas oil, gunshot, iron and lead piping, jute, manilla, paraffin, lampware, sulphuric and carbonic acid, textiles, beer and castor oil. At 3.23 pm on 21 February she was southeast of Iceland in strong winds and rough seas. Visibility was down to one mile when she encountered the cruiser *Manchester* and the destroyer *Kimberley*. A signal was flashed to the German freighter warning her crew that if they attempted to scuttle, they would be left to their fate. While *Kimberley* closed, *Manchester* reinforced the message with pompom fire close alongside the boats that had been launched. They were forced to return. One was left adrift, but the other was rehoisted because *Wahehe*'s stewardess could not climb up the side of the ship.

Kapitän Albers had no alternative but to set course for Kirkwall as instructed by Lieutenant-Commander Knowling in *Kimberley*. The German master tried to transmit, but his W/T signal was jammed by the destroyer, which also fired pompom bursts over *Wahehe*. It was not until the next afternoon that *Kimberley* was able to send a boarding party.

'Well, what are you going to do now—shoot us all?' asked Kapitän Albers (ADM1/10439: *German SS Wahehe*). He had apparently believed that *Manchester* was deliberately trying to hit *Wahehe*'s lifeboats. He was left with this assumption, but assured that no one would be shot—provided there was no trouble. There was no trouble and *Wahehe* anchored in Kirkwall on 24 February.

Orizaba was one of the Vigo ships which passed the Northern Patrol but for her, Norway proved a false security. She struck a rock off Skjervöy and was a total loss.

The 7768-ton *Wangoni*, the largest of this batch of Vigo vessels, reached and passed through Norwegian waters, but then encountered the British submarine *Triton* off Kristiansand. The passenger liner's luck did not desert her and she was able to make her escape during the night hours of 28 February.

North Atlantic nights would still be dark and stormy for another month or so, although the weather did not always co-operate with the blockade runners. Northern nights, even in midwinter, could be clear and full-moon bright while the sticky rain and fog which characterized some tropical areas could suddenly dissipate. However, before they could take advantage of any climatic camouflage, the blockade runners first had to break out, as was done on Leap Year Day, 29 February 1940, from Aruba.

There were in fact three German ships there: *Antilla*, *Troja* and *Heidelberg*. Captain J.V. Farquhar had seen their dark shapes silhouetted against the lights of Orangestadt the previous night. Twenty-four hours later, *Despatch*'s searchlight was illuminating a Dutch flag painted on the seaward side of a darkened ship just outside Dutch waters. Immediately fire broke out on the stranger and by the time the boarding party was alongside, she was listing to port, and her bridge was an inferno. Kapitän Boendel and his crew were taken on board the cruiser.

Despatch then looked into Aruba again and assumed that *Antilla* had taken advantage of *Troja's* self-sacrifice to escape. However, it was *Heidelberg* that had slipped out. She made it to the Windward Passage between Cuba and Hispaniola, and there on 2 March 1940 was *Dunedin*, transferred from the Northern Patrol. News of *Heidelberg's* scuttling was piped on board *Despatch* 'to the huge delight of the ship's company' (ADM1/10658: *Report of Proceedings from HMS Despatch*).

The Hansa freighter *Wolfsburg* disguised herself as the Norwegian *Aust* when coming from Pernambuco on 2 March. She was found by the cruiser *Berwick* hugging the Greenland ice far up in the Denmark Strait. In spite of being fired at by pompoms, Kapitän Bohland ordered his ship to be scuttled and abandoned. The boarding party got across very promptly and tried to smother the fire by covering the ventilators from the holds. The flames continued to spread through the cargo of general merchandise, while, in the engine room, water was reaching the underside of the cylinders. As *Wolfsburg* listed further to starboard, they gathered up whatever logs and used charts they could lay their hands on. The W/T office yielded up a heap of burnt paper and then they left her. British and German boats were hoisted aboard *Berwick* while *Wolfsburg* drifted onto the ice to be sunk by the cruiser's gunfire.

In the late afternoon of 5 March, the Hull Trawler *St Wistan* took a hand. She was fishing on the Arctic Circle northwest of Iceland when her skipper saw a vessel with American colours painted on her side. Their height above the waterline indicated that they had been applied at sea. The skipper then informed the Fishing Section Officer who was in wartime charge of the trawler without interfering with the actual business of catching fish. The two men decided that this was a neutral American blockade runner and made an appropriate signal by W/T. The skipper of *St Wistan* was later awarded £23 for keeping a good lookout, the wireless operator £10 and the seventeen hands £1 each. There was nothing for the RNR lieutenant—he was only doing his job—nor was there any publicity, for fear of German reprisals on the British fishing fleet.

Two hours later at 7 pm, *Berwick* had taken in the signal, and her navigating officer was working out the stranger's likeliest route. Next morning she was located by the cruiser's Walrus which was then recovered as snow began to fall with increasing wind and sea. At 4.35 pm a vessel was sighted three miles away. Although bearing the Moore McCormack name of *Argosy*, from Philadelphia, she broadcast an SOS as the Hamburg-Südamerika *Uruguay*. Partially jammed by the cruiser, the signal was repeated by Reykjavik, but then *Berwick* transmitted *Uruguay's* call-sign and said no further assistance was required. By now the German ship was being abandoned, in spite of overhead bursts from a Lewis gun. Again, the boarding party tried to deal with fires and flooding, but without success. It was believed that her cargo included manganese ore and she seemed about to capsize at any moment. After the boarders had returned to *Berwick* bearing documents and sextants, *Uruguay* was sunk with 4-inch (10.2-cm) gunfire. The Germans joined their compatriots in the seamen's recreation space. All were interrogated, with the usual crop of rumours about marvellous secret weapons. It was also learned that all ships remaining in South American harbours were laid up with engine defects—which may have been a deliberate attempt to misinform the British.

The last paragraph of Captain I.M. Palmer's report to Their Lords of the Admiralty read (ADM1/10593: *Interception of German Merchant Vessels*):

> An unfortunate incident occurred when the ship's Bulldog (male) showed marked interest in a captured Dachshund of the opposite sex. The Dachshund turned on him and he, with a complete disregard for the traditions of the service which he had (recently) joined, beat an undignified and hasty retreat.

A summary of the cruiser *York*'s *Report of Proceedings for March 1940* (ADM1/10624) shows that she was having an equally eventful patrol.

Friday, 1 March: Sailed from Scapa Flow.

Saturday, 2 March: On Northern Patrol line NP53.

Sunday, 3 March: Wind west-southwest, strong to gale force.

0915: Sighted merchantman about eight miles away in position 63°08′N/ 14°42′W.

1015: Fired .5-inch (12.7-mm) machine-gun across ship's bows and near a boat that had been launched to drive her back, but she could not return to the merchantman. Some men were still on board ship. Saw capsized boat. *York* went alongside this boat and tried to rescue men clinging to it, but not all could be saved. Other boat came alongside *York*, but impact with the cruiser's hull stove in the boat. Learned that ship was *Arucas* (last of the vessels to break out of Vigo). *Arucas* began making W/T signals which were jammed by *York*. *York* told those still on board *Arucas* that they would not be saved if their ship sank and ordered them to try to stop the leak with mattresses. Germans tried to comply by lowering one over the side to cover the condenser inlet, but failed. Full gale now blowing. *York* ordered Germans to abandon ship. Last five jumped overboard lashed together, but they had left too short a scope between each other. *York* could not pull them up singly and the line broke under the weight. Master, Kapitän Mohring, was lost in this way.

1915: *Arucas* on beam ends; opened fire to sink her before dark.

1950: *Arucas* foundered; ten missing, believed drowned; forty-three rescued, three of whom died later. Interrogation revealed that master did not intend to scuttle because weather too bad, but when he gave the order to stand by, the chief engineer opened and destroyed the seacocks; *Arucas* believed to be carrying hides, ore and sardines. She had been waiting off Greenland for the ice to clear and then tried to pass between Iceland and Faeroes.

Monday, 4 March: Visibility extreme; sighted mountains of Iceland 70 miles away.

1130: Funeral service for Germans; German crew gave Nazi salute as bodies committed.

Sighted AMC *Wolfe* en route to her patrol area. Sighted unidentified trawler making for Reykjavik at limit of extreme visibility.

Tuesday, 5 March: Weather very good. Closed and boarded outward-bound empty Norwegian tanker *Albert L. Ellsworth;* released her. Sighted and carried out range and inclination exercise with cruiser *Manchester*, then parted company. Sighted AMC *Derbyshire*. Sighted capsized lifeboat.

Wednesday, 6 March: Sighted *Derbyshire*.

Thursday, 7 March: Wind westerly, strong to gale force.

Friday, 8 March: Wind northwest, strong; sea rough. Sighted *Manchester*.

2000: Intercepted Norwegian *Haalweg* from Newport News to Aalesund.

2042: Informed Vice-Admiral Northern Patrol that *York* proceeding in company without diverting *Haalweg*, who said that his cargo of coal was covered by Navicert A.1531. 'CAN SHIP BE RELEASED.'

Saturday, 9 March: 0430: 'TO YORK. FROM VANP. YOUR 2042/8. YES.' Parted company with *Haalweg*. Later left patrol line. Sighted AMCs *Cilicia* and *Circassia* and trawler *Northern Sun*.

Sunday, 10 March: Arrived Kirkwall.

Now, the scene again changed to the Caribbean. Until 5 March, the Dutch island of Curaçao had harboured the NDL banana and passenger cargo-liner *Hannover*. On that date she slipped out, her two-shaft diesels driving her through the waves at 15 knots. Allied commanders made their dispositions. On the night of 7/8 March, on the western side of Mona Passage between the islands of Hispaniola and Puerto Rico, *Dunedin* found her. Kapitän Wahnschaff made for neutral Dominican waters, but the Canadian destroyer *Assiniboine* was also coming up. Their crews were determined not to let this prize escape them, even though she was seen to be on fire. In hot pursuit, *Dunedin* came alongside, fire-fighting parties clambered over, and a tow was rigged. They pulled *Hannover* well clear of territorial waters, closed the seacocks, put the fire out and towed her to Jamaica, where she arrived four days later. The Germans would hear of her again—as *Audacity*, the world's first escort carrier.

Under cover of this excitement, two more ships had left Curaçao, only a few hours after *Hannover*. They were *Mimi Horn* and *Seattle*. Both freighters cleared the Caribbean and *Seattle* reached Tromso on 31 March, but the 4007-ton *Mimi Horn* did not evade the Northern Patrol. She was sighted at a distance of 15 miles by *Transylvania* on 28 March. She set herself on fire and was obviously a total loss by the time the AMC arrived.

This fate had already befallen *La Coruna* on 13 March. Coming from Rio de Janeiro, this Hamburg-Südamerika freighter was steering east between Iceland and the Faeroes when challenged by the AMC *Maloja* during the Forenoon Watch. She gave her name as the Japanese *Taki Maru*, and took advantage of a heavy snowstorm to turn 90 degrees to port, heading north at full speed. Her respite was shortlived. The flurry of snow cleared as suddenly as it had begun and *Maloja* gave chase. Soon the AMC was overhauling *La Coruna* and ordering her to stop. A shell across her bows was more effective, and she hove-to. *Maloja*'s boarding party set out, but before they had reached *La Coruna*, a jet of steam showed that she was blowing off her boilers, usually a sign that the master has finished with engines. Then fires broke out forward and aft and the crew began lowerng the boats. The AMC recovered all eighteen officers and fifty men from two boats and finished off the derelict with gunfire. It was bad luck for *La Coruna*. She had already passed right through the Denmark Strait, but had encountered so much ice that she had turned back. Retracing his course, *La Coruna*'s master had decided to try a more southerly route to Norway.

The Germans were the subject of considerable debate on *Maloja*'s messdecks. A crew of sixty-eight seemed far too big for a 7221-ton merchantman—and they were more tidily dressed than the usual run of merchant seamen. One was rumoured to be a Gestapo agent and the 'buzz' went round that they were survivors from *Admiral Graf Spee*, released from Argentinian internment to return to the Fatherland. Their arrogant manner was also remembered long after they had been landed as prisoners at Gourock, especially their assertion that Germany would finish the war by Christmas 1940. The men of the Northern Patrol were not to know that many of the sailors from German blockade runners which were intercepted during this period were later sent to Canada aboard the ill-fated *Arandora Star*.

To prevent a breakout by seventeen German merchantmen in the Dutch East Indies, a special Malaya Force was created, consisting of three cruisers, two destroyers, two submarines and a sloop. Altogether 246 German merchant ships were lurking in neutral or friendly harbours around the world in April 1940. Fifty-eight ships had been captured or sunk, including those detained in Allied berths at the beginning of hostilities. Besides their cargoes, a further 558,857 tons of material had been seized from neutral vessels including twenty bags of coffee for the Führer's personal entourage. Another 3,600,000 tons of goods had been denied by means of the navicert system. However, in spite of its well-publicized successes, economic blockade had failed to bring Germany to her knees. Even the ubiquitous Royal Navy had not prevented the arrival of the majority of ships attempting a homeward run. Eighty-two vessels had reached Germany safely, some in ballast, but most contributing their cargoes to the Nazi war effort.

For example, Hamburg-Südamerika's 4117-ton *Bahia* departed her name port on 5 January 1940 and arrived at Narvik on 6 February, going on to deliver 1705 tons of cotton-seed cake, 1518 tons of cotton, 675 tons of wood pulp, 518 tons of chrome, 394 tons manganese ore, 258 tons coffee, 105 tons powdered horn, 10 tons gas oil, 3 tons rags, and 45 tons miscellaneous items.

One of those which had not yet unloaded her cargo was Hapag's *Seattle*, entering Kristiansandfjord at 6.23 am on 9 April 1940. As the fog cleared, her master could see the shapes of cruisers, torpedo boats and S-boats ahead of him— a German task force. Norwegian batteries opened fire; the German warships were shooting back. Overhead was the Luftwaffe. In their eyes, anything that was not part of the invasion fleet was hostile—and that included *Seattle*. Bombed and afire, shelled by the Norwegian destroyer *Gyller*, *Seattle* went down. The invasion of Norway had begun.

8 France and Italy

The dramatic offensives in the spring and summer of 1940 completely changed contraband control and blockade running. Now all the resources of Europe were at Axis disposal. To German mineral wealth and Italian foodstuffs were added Polish lead and fodder, Czech antimony, and an annual import of 500,000 tons of fish from Norway for food fertilizer and chemical manufacture. There were Danish and Dutch dairy products, Belgian wool, Luxembourg steel and French coal. All could be obtained on very favourable terms. The gun was always in the background, no matter how friendly the personal relationship between defeated and victorious businessmen. From Scandinavia, neutral and occupied, came 11,000,000 tons of iron ore a year. There was wolfram from Spain and sardines from Portugal. Soon the supply of bauxite and copper from Yugoslavia, petroleum from Rumania, sunflower seed oil from Bulgaria and chrome from Greece would be ensured by the occupation or enforced collaboration of those countries. Then it would be time to seize and exploit the oil and wheat of Russia. In the meantime, ignorant of their fate, the Soviets co-operated unstintingly with the Axis Nazis' New Economic Order, delivering 4,541,205 tons of material from 1939 to 1941. In addition, 28,820 tons of rubber and another 459,738 tons of other Oriental products came over the Trans-Siberian railway.

This economic cornucopia coincided with an improvement in Axis oceanic communications. The entire coastline of Europe from North Cape to Spain was under German domination or influence. The British declared the whole area a blockaded zone, but it afforded many more boltholes for Axis blockade runners. The ports of western France cut their voyage around Iceland (now a British base) by 2000 miles. German-occupied Europe also provided new bases for aircraft and U-boats, which reached out far into the Atlantic, keeping distant the Royal Navy's blockading warships and striking at Britain's own sea routes.

This was at the very time that the Royal Navy had sustained serious damage and had lost the assistance of the French Fleet, while commitments had been further extended by Italy's entry into the war, with consequent operations in the Mediterranean and Red Sea. In 1939, Italy's merchant marine had numbered 1235 ships, about a third of the total tonnage being trapped outside the Mediterranean when Mussolini announced that Italy would commence hostilities from midnight on 10 June 1940. From then on instructions to Italian merchant ships on the high seas came from Supermarina (Naval High Command) rather than from the Ministero delle Communicazioni.

The early experiences of Italian merchant seamen were similar to their German counterparts nine months before, although the current atmosphere of wartime Europe meant that masters were not taken completely by surprise. *Romolo* cleared Brisbane on 5 June, being promptly shadowed by the Australian *Manoora*. After four days the AMC was ordered to Singapore, an instruction that was reversed when the Italian had been out of sight for several hours. However, she was reported again in the Torres Strait and when *Manoora* sighted her for the second time, *Romolo* was scuttled.

Umbria's master was equally prompt. Detained in the Red Sea and escorted into Port Sudan on 9 June, he opened the seacocks as soon as he learned that his country was declaring war. This occasioned certain consternation in the port area, as *Umbria*'s cargo consisted of bombs, shells and fulminate of mercury for detonators. It was not until interrogation had revealed that no demolition charges had been ignited, that salvage crews could work without fear of booby-traps. By then *Umbria* was sinking fast and soon only her masts and funnel were above the surface.

Both *Timavo* and *Gerusalemme* sailed from Durban during the night of 9/10 June, but they could only be shadowed until South Africa's declaration took effect in the early hours of 11 June. That morning a strafing Blenheim forced *Timavo*'s crew to run her aground five miles north of St Mary's Hill. A similar fate befell *Gerusalemme*, intercepted by the AMC *Ranchi*. Ashore near Oro Point in Portuguese waters, she could not be touched. Later *Gerusalemme*'s crew got her off again and steamed her to Lourenço Marques where her communications equipment was used to relay reports from Axis agents working in South Africa.

The Italian colonies in East Africa afforded shelter for a number of vessels. Their cargoes were useful additions to local armament if they consisted of military stores, but strategic raw materials thus bottled up were denied to Italian factories as surely as if they had been sunk. The only Italian vessels that stood any chance of getting home in June 1940 were those already in the Mediterranean. Even here, Italian masters were at first left virtually to their own devices. Supermarina's prewar plans envisaged the creation and defence of sea corridors from Italy to Libya and the Dodecanese, fenced in by minefields and the fleet—not the operation of protected convoys. Such a policy soon proved impracticable and the first convoy sailed from Naples to Tripoli on 25 June 1940.

The Royal Navy's established examination centres at Gibraltar and Port Said completely sealed off Italy from neutral trans-ocean traffic. For a few more months, British cruisers and destroyers undertook occasional sweeps into the Aegean to intercept contraband passing through the Dardanelles. Then the invasion of Greece and the Axis aerial domination of the Aegean and much of the eastern Mediterranean brought such operations to an end. Cargoes of chrome, copper and other Anatolian products could be moved in comparative safety from neutral Turkey through Greek waters and the Corinth Canal, and up the Adriatic, joining the raw materials from Yugoslavia.

Allied pressure tried to control this traffic at source, but this was not completely accomplished until 2 August 1944, when Turkey broke off diplomatic relations with Germany, declaring war on 23 February 1945. Nor, until then, with the Red Army advancing into the Balkans, could there be any interference with rail and riverine transport in the area, although maritime trade via the Dardanelles and the Aegean had been severely disrupted since the middle of 1943. This coastal shipment of raw materials was undoubtedly important to Axis industry, but most merchant ship activity on both sides in the Mediterranean was closely connected with military operations.

Meanwhile the establishment of Vichy France had created a fresh neutral state within Germany's orbit, but which depended upon overseas cargoes from her colonies. From Africa came fruit, vegetables and wheat, ground nuts for edible oils and cattle cake, phosphates for fertilizers. And there was rubber from the Far East. Britain feared that if this trade continued unabated, then much contraband would find its way to the Axis powers. On the other hand, influential American opinion did not want the children of France and other occupied countries to starve. The various diplomatic arguments were reflected in the instructions given to Royal Navy warships concerning the interception of Vichy French merchantmen.

Generally they were only to be stopped if unescorted and outside neutral territorial waters. French ships on passage between Marseilles and Dakar could spend most of the Mediterranean and part of the African portions of their voyage in Spanish waters, although there were places where navigational hazards could force them well out to sea. From 7 September 1940, the French Navy tried to provide escort on sections where interception was likely. Over the next two years, a total of 1750 French merchantmen passed in convoys between Casablanca and Oran.

They, and vessels proceeding directly from North Africa, delivered 4,400,000 tons of cargo to Metropolitan France. In October 1940, the British Admiralty announced that they would not allow Vichy warships to proceed beyond Dakar, thus preventing interference with Gaullist territories. However, those sloops already in the Indian Ocean and Far East were employed as escorts for small convoys of rubber and other raw materials from Indo-China via Madagascar.

These sloops were not to open fire first; their job was to reply to British communications and handle any incidents which occurred. Later, Royal Navy officers were ordered to intercept protected as well as unescorted Vichy merchantmen, although they were also instructed to avoid the use of force whenever possible. An overwhelming and facesaving show of strength was better than opening fire. Detained ships were usually 'requisitioned,' that procedure being considered less aggressive than seizing them as prizes, even when the latter was justified by technical resistance such as attempted scuttling or sabotage. Officers, crew and passengers were temporarily interned as prohibited immigrants, and not permanently incarcerated as prisoners of war.

On the other side, the Germans naturally imposed their own conditions before allowing the resumption of French trade. In particular, they insisted that French masters scuttle their vessels if intercepted by the Royal Navy. However, Contre-Amiral (Rear-Admiral) Paul Auphan, responsible for the Mercantile Department of the French Navy Ministry, promulgated written orders that ships were to be scuttled only if the crews were not endangered. After that, token resistance usually took the form of token sabotage. Altogether the Royal Navy stopped 104 French merchantmen. Four were scuttled and forty-three released. The remainder were seized by Britain, although several were recaptured by Vichy warships or by their own crews. The story is told of one prize crew on board the trawler *Joseph Elise* who were plied with wine until in a suitable state to be locked away while the Frenchmen took their ship to Casablanca.

The first interceptions of Vichy French ships on the high seas were involved with the Anglo-Free French expedition to Dakar in September 1940. The oiler *Tarn* was turned back to Casablanca and the freighter *Touareg* was captured by the cruiser *Dragon*, while *Poitiers* and her general cargo of 1700 tons was sunk by the cruiser *Cumberland*'s gunfire after her crew had set her on fire.

Later in the year, in November, some merchantmen were being run from the French colonies direct to the Biscay shores of Occupied France. This traffic could hardly be said to benefit civilians in the Unoccupied Zone and its prevention became one of the responsibilities of Force H at Gibraltar. The measures taken helped to convince the Vichy government of the impracticability of these shipments.

Warships based at Gibraltar were also invloved in the interception of convoys from Casablanca to Oran and Marseilles. On New Year's Day 1941, five British destroyers stopped such a convoy escorted by a single armed trawler off the North African coast. Two out of the four merchantmen were empty tankers and their acquisition was a valuable addition to the type of vessel in service with the British Merchant Navy. The passenger ship, *Chantilly*, tried to make for territorial waters, but was headed off and stopped by *Jaguar*. The two ships lay close together, *Jaguar* on the liner's starboard quarter. Their position was continually checked to make sure they did not drift into territorial waters. For three-quarters of an hour, the destroyer's motor-boat circled *Chantilly* looking for a means of boarding, while a slop pail was hung over the side as a suitable receptacle for British communications. At last an accommodation ladder was rigged, but the French master, Capitaine Corinwinder, descended the steps and got in the way of the British boarding officer who pushed past him.

Lieutenant-Commander Hine had been watching this from *Jaguar*'s bridge. *Chantilly*'s decks were crowded with passengers, including French servicemen. They were obviously unfriendly and resentful, while many were wearing life-belts, which suggested that the ship was about to be scuttled. They could also have concealed weapons and looked as if they were about to overwhelm the British boarding party. A stronger warning than signals and a loudhailer was needed. Lieutenant-Commander Hine walked to the rear of *Jaguar*'s bridge and leaned over to call out to the Port .5-inch (12.7-mm) quadruple mounting just below him. He pointed approximately Red 135 degrees, well clear of *Chantilly*'s stern, said 'Fire a burst into the water on the bearing' (ADM1/18914: *Madame Tart*), and resumed his study of the liner.

Although *Jaguar* was at Action Stations with some weapons trained and loaded, the guns' crews had not been ordered to close up in the firing position. This particular mounting *had* closed up, without waiting for the order. It was also trained on Red 45 degrees, pointing just forward of *Chantilly*'s accommoda-tion ladder. The leading seaman captain of the gun was staring at the French ship through binoculars, which he should not have been doing as he had not been detailed as a lookout. As soon as the able seaman gunlayer heard Lieutenant-Commander Hine's voice, and without waiting for the order to be correctly relayed via the captain of the gun, he depressed the mounting and fired. Eight rounds splashed into the water and ricocheted upwards. Monsieur Tart (Chef du Cabinet de Gouverneur de Madagascar) and his twelve-year old daughter both died with multiple bullet wounds. One woman was blinded in the left eye and three men were wounded in the legs or arms. A momentary panic was halted by the French master and the boarding party who also searched for scuttling charges and secured the W/T transmitter. Extra hands came from *Duncan* and *Jaguar*'s medical officer was ferried over.

At first the French officers were very bitter—'This is another blot on the name of the British Navy' (ADM1/18914: *Madame Tart*)—but gradually they ap-preciated that it had been an accident and all the fault of the war. The wounded were particularly forgiving while the widow, Madame Tart, refused to co-operate in any anti-British propaganda. During the ensuing diplomatic ex-changes, the British government pointed out that 'this regrettable accident arose, not from any act of aggression on the behalf of His Majesty's ship, but from the resistance of the Master and Chief Officer of the S.S. "Chantilly" to a perfectly legitimate operation' (quoted from *Madame Tart*).

In any case the payment of compensation could be a precedent for all sorts of damage caused by wartime mistakes and accidents in the heat and tension of battle or crisis. These arguments were repeated in 1945, but later the sum of £500 was forwarded to Madame Tart via naval channels. The incident was but one of the 55 million tragedies of World War II.

The largest capture of Vichy French merchant ships occurred in November 1941 and was known as Operation Bellringer. Three months earlier South African armed trawlers had attempted to intercept a French convoy passing the Cape of Good Hope, but they had lost touch during the night. This time, two cruisers, two AMCs, six minesweeping trawlers and four Martin Maryland bombers were deployed. The convoy was sighted, shadowed and surrounded at dawn on 3 November. There was an exchange of signals between the cruiser *Devonshire* and the sloop *d'Iberville*, and both ships trained their guns on each other. Anxious to avoid bloodshed, *d'Iberville* signalled the five merchantmen to do as they were bidden by the British and then set course back to Madagascar, while the French merchant crews did what they could to damage their ships before the English got hold of them. *Cap Padaran* was immobilized and had to be taken in tow by the AMC *Carthage*. *Bangkok* (which had delivered 3000 tons of rubber to Casablanca six months before) was set on fire and abandoned. The cruiser *Colombo* opened fire with a machine-gun, the bullets raking the water just ahead of the lifeboats, until the survivors scrambled back aboard, where they had no alternative but to put out the blaze themselves. The other captures were *Compiègne*, *Florida* and *Commandant Dorise*. All were brought into South African ports. Their cargo included 900 tons of graphite and 30,000 tons of rice.

This was the last commercial voyage undertaken by French merchantmen. From now on small cargoes were transported by sloops and submarines: nothing like the voyage of *Francois L.D.* She had sailed from Indo-China with 6600 tons of rubber, ostensibly for Japan, but she bunkered in the Philippines, proceeded across the Pacific and rounded Cape Horn to unload at Casablanca. The British considered intercepting such journeys in the East Indies, but the Far Eastern war prevented any more such activity by either party in this sideshow of the economic war.

9 The Prizes Return

By the late summer of 1940, the Royal Navy was so widely dispersed that German raiders could operate with impunity in the remoter oceans. Most merchantmen they encountered were sunk, but some modern, economically fast vessels with valuable cargoes were retained as prizes. After some time as auxiliary warships, supply tenders or in hiding in the Antarctic, they set out for France. The first was *Krossfonn*, a Norwegian tanker captured in the central Atlantic by the raider *Widder* on 26 June 1940.

The first to attempt the long passage from the southern hemisphere was *Tropic Sea*, another Norwegian motor vessel, this time a freighter with 8101 tons of Australian wheat for Britain. From 19 to 30 June *Tropic Sea* (now sometimes referred to as *Kurmark*, after the original name of her captor, *Orion*) prepared for her dangerous voyage from the South Pacific. Forty prisoners from the British *Haxby* were accommodated on board as well as the Norwegians. False papers were provided and arrangements made for scuttling. Extra provisions and engine spares were transferred plus 300 tons of diesel. When asked what he would do if he ran short of fuel, the officer commanding the prize crew replied tersely that he would rig sails. That was typical of Kapitän Steinkrauss. He had served as a rating in the Kaiser's High Seas Fleet and had then joined the German merchant navy. At the beginning of World War II, he was commanding the old tanker *Winnetou*, sheltering at Las Palmas. SKL ordered him to act as *Orion*'s supply oiler, although her stationary months in the Canaries had enabled a luxuriant marine growth to take hold, which often cut *Winnetou*'s speed to 4 knots, her late arrival at secret meeting places being foreshadowed by masses of funnel smoke. Nor was she properly equipped for fuelling at sea.

Kapitän Steinkrauss coped with every problem, emphasizing his civilian status by replying to requests from Kriegsmarine officers with a dour 'All right' —in English. Inevitably he was known as 'Kapitän Allright.' All raiders carried extra personnel to man prizes. They were usually officers and ratings with mercantile experience, or were time-expired reservists who had been recalled to service. However, *Tropic Sea*'s voyage required someone of special experience so Kapitän Steinkrauss was given a temporary reserve commission (a Sonder-führer) commanding a prize crew of eleven Kriegsmarine and seventeen mercantile sailors. *Winnetou* remained in the Far East with *Orion* cheering *Tropic Sea*'s departure. Twice in July 1940, her estimated route was transmitted by *Orion* to SKL via Japanese wireless and the German Naval Attaché in Tokyo. *Tropic Sea* proceeded round Cape Horn and then northwards. Approaching Europe on 3 September 1940, her track crossed that of the British submarine *Truant*.

Lieutenant-Commander Haggard (nephew of the novelist Rider Haggard) was looking out for suitable targets while crossing the Bay of Biscay en route to the Mediterranean. This solitary Norwegian-looking vessel aroused his suspicions and he ordered her to stop. There was no escape and there was no point in sacrificing lives. Kapitän Steinkrauss told everybody to abandon ship and blew the scuttling charges. Somehow Lieutenant-Commander Haggard's sixty-man crew found room in their 265-foot submarine for the *Haxby* British, plus the Norwegian master and his wife. Kapitän Steinkrauss was also brought on board, but after a while he was returned to the lifeboats accommodating his own men and the rest of the Norwegians. Meanwhile *Tropic Sea* was not sinking very quickly. The scuttling charges had blown a 10-foot hole in her side, but the Norwegians might be able to repair that rent. The master was not keen on the idea. *Tropic Sea* had only enough fuel for another 400 miles left in her bunkers, and there were four more demolition charges still on board. During this discussion the sea was still seeping in, causing the grain to swell, straining seams, popping rivets, lifting plates, and allowing more water in. *Tropic Sea* was suddenly visibly sinking deeper and deeper and in two minutes she was gone. *Truant* therefore departed leaving the lifeboats on a fairly calm sea and not too far from the coast.

Next day, a Sunderland flying boat landed and picked up the Norwegians, while the Germans made their way towards France, their plight being signalled to their authorities after *Truant* had disembarked her passengers at Gibraltar. A storm then swept away the lifeboat's mast and sails, so that the German seamen had to resort to oars. It took them several days to row to Spain, whence they crossed over into Occupied France. Kapitän Steinkrauss flew to Berlin, his first home visit for four years, but he was soon on his travels again, catching trains through Poland and Russia back to the Far East where he would take command of the tanker *Benno*, formerly the Norwegian *Ole Jacob*, one of *Atlantis*' prizes.

Back on 10 June 1940, *Atlantis* had taken yet another Norwegian vessel, *Tirranna*. Her cargo, intended for Egypt and the Australian troops there, included 3000 tons of wheat, 6000 bales of wool, 178 trucks, 5500 cases of beer, 300 cases of tobacco, 3000 cases of peaches, 17,000 cases of jam and 5000 pairs of socks. She was so obviously Norwegian that she stood a good chance of being accepted as genuine by British warships. In fact, her greatest danger might come from U-boats taking appropriate action against her. Accordingly, as soon as *Tirranna* had set out from the Indian Ocean on 5 August 1940, *Atlantis* hurried a thousand miles away to inform SKL of the prize's identity and course.

After just two days of lonely passage, *Tirranna* sighted—and evaded—a British cruiser. The prize crew had already decided that if challenged they would surrender immediately. By now, *Tirranna* was also carrying ninety-five European prisoners of war and interned civilian men, women and children of various nationalities, plus 179 Indian seamen. However, nothing happened, not even as they entered the designated blockade area around western Europe. Lifejackets were worn continuously as they passed the Spanish coast and hove-to about three miles off the Gironde estuary on 21 September 1940. A French fishing boat took one of the German officers ashore to contact Naval Group West. Admittedly, the organization had not been established long. Local headquarters at Bordeaux were having to make arrangements for the arrival of an Italian submarine flotilla (Betasom) from the Mediterranean, at the same time as priority was being given to the preparations for Operation Seelöwe farther north. Perhaps some people were still affected by the euphoria of victory over France. What was one captured merchant ship more or less? Their attitude seemed to confirm the seafarer's traditional opinion of shore staff efficiency through the ages. When the prize officer eventually did get through to the right person, he was told that *Tirranna* could not yet enter the Gironde and proceed 62 miles upriver to Bordeaux because the RAF might have laid mines in the channel. Minesweepers were being sent and would arrive tomorrow morning. What did another twelve hours matter when *Tirranna* had come halfway round the world? Yes, the British had declared the Bay of Biscay a 'sink at sight' zone, but there were no submarines in this area.

There was no sign of the minesweepers at dawn, nor during the forenoon. There was no sign of the minesweepers, as fussed over by stewards, the civilian passengers dozed and sunned themselves under a calm blue sky. There was no sign of the minesweepers just after lunchtime, when four torpedoes struck *Tirranna*'s dark grey hull. Three exploded. *Tirranna* rolled over and went down in seven minutes in a babel of confused languages, buoyant wreckage hurtling to the surface and smashing into those who had survived the actual sinking. All helped each other; a British doctor turned a raft into a bobbing casualty ward. A Luftwaffe aircraft flew over and a warship came to the rescue. Presently, the minesweepers arrived. Out to sea the British submarine *Tuna* slid into deeper water to reload her tubes. Sixty-one people had lost their lives.

The risks had to be run. Raider captains were rebuked if they scuttled suitable prizes instead of sending them back in an attempt to run the blockade to an Axis port. Sometimes the gamble paid off, but with little dividend. The twenty-seven year-old *Durmitor*, a Yugoslav tramp steamer, was captured by *Atlantis* in the Indian Ocean on 22 October 1940. She was technically neutral, and neither the ship nor her cargo of salt was of any use to the raider. Accordingly she was despatched to Italian East Africa, carrying three hundred prisoners, who shared a wire cage on the salt with hordes of rats. Short of water, with relieving squalls of rain turning the hard salt to slush, with the prisoners near mutiny, with firemen burning furniture and barely flammable clots of paint and ashes, and with primitive sails rigged, *Durmitor* lurched across the ocean swell at a bare 3 knots to run aground at Uarsciek. While the prisoners formed the centrepiece of a triumphal procession through Mogadishu, the prize crew and the Yugoslavs refloated *Durmitor*—twice—so that she could stagger into Mogadishu, 50 miles down the coast. Making a prominent, undamaged target, she could well provoke another British bombardment, so off she went again, this time to Kismayu, almost on the Kenyan border. The place would soon be under British assault.

Sometimes the gamble succeeded beyond all expectation. In just forty-eight January hours of Antarctic stalking, *Pinguin* captured the Norwegian whale factory ships *Ole Wegger*, *Solglimt* and *Pelagos* together with their whalecatchers *Star XIV*, *Star XIX*, *Star XX*, *Star XXI*, *Star XXII*, *Star XXIII*, *Star XXIV*, *Pol VIII*, *Pol IX*, *Pol X* and *Torlyn*. Their cargoes totalled 10,300 tons of fuel oil and 20,500 tons of whale oil. The latter was an important ingredient of margarine, while the whalecatchers would make ideal patrol craft. Kapitän zür See Kruder informed SKL of his haul and it was decided to send them all to Bordeaux —except *Pol IX*, retained as an auxiliary minelayer. *Pelagos* and *Solglimt* departed the Antarctic on 25 January 1941, while *Ole Wegger* and five pairs of catchers followed from the South Atlantic on 18 February 1941.

Arrangements were made for the shortlegged craft to fuel en route from *Spichern* (formerly *Krossfonn*), sent out from France to meet them and the raider *Thor* southwest of the Azores. *Star XIX* and *Star XXIV* were intercepted by the sloop *Scarborough* and scuttled themselves. All the rest, eight catchers preceded by three whale factory ships, reached Bordeaux safely. It was a remarkable achievement, contrasting with the experience of *Gneisenau*'s prizes which had less distance to cover at the same time of year. On 15 March 1941, during her sortie with *Scharnhorst*, she had captured three unescorted tankers. They were despatched to Brest, but five days later, two of them were sighted by Swordfish from *Ark Royal*, out hunting the enemy battlecruisers. Surface ships of Force H were guided to the scene, but as soon as they came in sight, the Germans scuttled *San Casimiro* and *Bianca*. The Norwegian *Polykarp*, however, was undetected and reached the Gironde. She was later renamed *Taifun*, being employed as a naval supply oiler.

The episode shows that prizes stood a better chance of survival if they could be held in a safe area until the hue and cry over their disappearance had died down. Vital convoy routes and associated naval activity meant that there could be few suitable places in the North Atlantic. Those that did exist were utilized as fuelling rendezvous for surface and submarine raiders. It was not a good idea to draw attention to them by having several ships lingering there for several weeks at a time, as could be done in the vast expanses of the southern hemisphere. *Nordvard*, *Kertosono*, *Storstad* and *Sandefjord* were among the prizes which made a successful passage to Europe.

Raider captains showed great ingenuity in utilizing the cargoes of captured merchantmen, but such expediencies were no substitute for regular supplies of stores and fuel. It had been to meet this situation that the Emergency Naval Supply Service had been secretly established before the war began. Those vessels sheltering in the Far East were best situated. The conclusion of the Three-Power Pact on 27 September 1940 meant that the Japanese, though still neutral, were again feeling friendlier towards the Nazis. They took little notice of German ships with Red Suns painted on their funnels in the mandated islands of the Marshalls and the Carolines. Captured cargoes were exchanged in return for suitable fuel for the raiders. *Regensburg* and *Kulmerland*, both thinly disguised as *Tokyo Maru*, sailed from Kobe, delivering full loads of oil, stores, provisions, drinking water and iced beer to lonely Pacific anchorages. Both also served as unarmed scouting vessels, rescued survivors and returned to Japan with intelligence reports for Admiral Wenneker's onward transmission from Tokyo.

Other merchantmen were also involved in this shuttle service. Some had been in Japan since the beginning of the war, while others proceeded thither from other Pacific ports, including South America; but not the 9179-ton *Weser*. Ordered to meet *Orion*, she was captured by the Canadian AMC *Prince Robert* near Manzanillo on 26 September 1940. On the Atlantic shore, ships were being ordered by SKL to take advantage of the northern winter, repeating the bockade running efforts of twelve months before. The freighter *Helgoland* departed Puerto Colombia at the head of the Gulf of Darien on 24 October 1940. The ubiquitous American destroyers set off in pursuit, but *Helgoland* evaded them, made her way past the island of St Thomas and disappeared into the Atlantic. On 30 November 1940, she was entering St Nazaire.

The US Navy's watch off Tampico was tighter. No less than four German freighters—*Orinoco*, *Phrygia*, *Idarwald* and *Rhein*—attempted a breakout. They were immediately observed by American destroyers, whose behaviour was such that *Phrygia*'s master believed that they were Royal Navy ships and ordered his vessel to be scuttled. The others were unable to shake off their shadowers, and by dawn on 15 November they were back at their berths. On 29 November two tried again, keeping close to the Mexican shore as far as the Yucatan Channel. They were trailed by two American destroyers, they and their reliefs broadcasting the customary series of position reports. These enabled the British cruiser *Diomede* to intercept the 5033-ton *Idarwald* just south of Cuba on 8 December.

The Germans opened and smashed the seacocks and set fire to their ship. Their lifeboats bobbed gently on the calm Caribbean as *Diomede* went straight alongside her quarry. A boarding party leapt across, hoses were passed over and the fires in the freighter's bridge and after superstructure extinguished. Choking smoke billowed up from smouldering coal bunkers, but these too were damped down, as much by rising seawater as by *Diomede*'s efforts. When it became too dark to work, the cruiser cast off, returning to *Idarwald* next morning. By now, the freighter had settled much lower in the water. A tow was rigged, but she was too far gone. Again *Diomede* slipped and there was a jetting mist of explosive spray from *Idarwald*'s forecastle as her forward bulkhead gave way. She sank soon afterwards.

Meanwhile, *Rhein* (of 6031 tons) had steered north of Cuba, heading through the Straits of Florida. Here were sailors of yet another nationality—Dutchmen, in their purposeful sloop *Van Kinsbergen*. At 25½ knots, she was the fastest of her type in the world. She could not be outrun and her captain intended to board. *Rhein*'s master recognized there was no escape and set his ship on fire. The damage was irreparable and when the cruiser *Caradoc* arrived, all that the British could do was sink the derelict with 6-inch (15.2-cm) gunfire on 11 December 1940.

Most blockade runners which broke out successfully and subsequently met raiders in mid-ocean took on board prisoners from the warships for transport to camps in Germany. Conditions on board were usually bad, food and water being severely rationed. A variety of nationalities (not all of whom were opposed to German victory) were crammed into cargo holds, spending the last fortnight of the voyage battened down. *Portland*, coming from Valparaiso and meeting *Nordmark* in the South Atlantic, experienced rather different incidents amongst her 327 prisoners.

Merchant seamen were civilians and the duty of escape and of hindering the enemy's war effort was not laid upon them as upon sailors under martial discipline. Nor were they expected to display any particular loyalty to their service once their ship had gone down. Not until 1941 were British merchant seamen guaranteed pay after being shipwrecked or captured, although some companies did pay employees' wages in such circumstances before this law was passed.

On board *Portland*, however, was Able Seaman Arthur Fry, formerly of *Afric Star*, and a man of considerable resource and determination. He enlisted the aid of Able Seamen Lynch and Merrett, and together they worked out a plan for overpowering the German officer when he made his rounds last thing at night. They would then take over the ship and sail her to England. This scheme was vetoed by the British officer in charge of the prisoners, after informers leaked a warning to the Germans. They then decided the best way of attracting the attention of a Royal Navy warship would be to set the ship on fire while passing through the Bay of Biscay. This they did, but their captors managed to put it out even before anybody knew anything was amiss. There was a party of Royal Navy ratings in the hold, but their officer, who was being held separately, had instructed them to stand by and await his orders.

Next morning, the lights failed suddenly and accidentally, whereupon the Kriegsmarine guard on duty in the hold fired his automatic pistol into the prisoners sitting in front of him, wounding two men, one of them fatally. After *Portland*'s arrival at Bordeaux on 14 March 1941, SS men came on board and for sixty hours interrogated and beat up the prisoners, concentrating on the Royal Navy ratings. Later Able Seamen Fry, Lynch and Merrett were taken to Hamburg and tried for mutiny and arson. The ringleader was sentenced to death, the others to imprisonment. However, Able Seaman Fry, who took all the responsibility for the incidents, was not executed and all three survived the war to receive the British Empire Medal.

10 The Indian Ocean

For the Italians in 1940, Bab el Mandeb, separating the Red Sea from the Indian Ocean, was indeed a Gate of Woe. Just ten miles wide, it was usually firmly closed by British warships to prevent any intercourse between Eritrea, Ethiopia and Italian Somaliland, coastal shipping being the only practical form of transport because of deserts and mountains. It was not only large ships which were stopped. Big cruisers, bristling with guns, bore down on small dhows, so that the lateen sails drooped in the lee of the steel bulk and the wooden vessel hove-to involuntarily. If carrying contraband—and virtually all of them were, 500 tons at most—than an armed guard was put on board to share the life of the Arab crew and ensure they steered for Aden. So many vessels were seized, that eventually the Italian colonists and their subject peoples in Massawa faced starvation. There was similar privation in Vichy French Djibouti, also blockaded from the sea because of its metre-gauge railway to Addis Ababa. Djibouti was suspected by both sides, and it was in an attempt to threaten the French, that the Italian army captured Berbera in British Somaliland in August 1940. This success proved of no benefit, because of British control of the sea. Not a single Italian loss of men or *matériel* could be replaced from without. Nevertheless these Italian sallyports did pose something of a threat to British communications. Their assault could only be a matter of time. When that happened the Italian and German merchantmen sheltering there would either have to be scuttled or take their chances at sea.

Kapitän Steuer, master of the 7840-ton *Tannenfels*, did not wait for that to happen. His ship, owned by DDG Hansa and at Kismayu, was only three years old, her twin six-cylinder diesel coupled to a single shaft giving her a speed of 16 knots. The prize crew from the unfortunate *Durmitor* came on board and *Tannenfels* sailed on 31 January 1941. Ten days later British warships cordoned off Kismayu and Mogadishu, while the 12th African Division launched its offensive from Kenya into Italian Somaliland. Kismayu was nearest that attack and that night, ten Axis merchantmen tried to escape. Depending on the fuel in their bunkers, they hoped to reach neutral Diego Suarez in Madagascar or, failing that, Mogadishu 250 miles farther away from the British advance. They had left it too late.

The carrier *Hermes* had arrived off the coast. Vigilant aircraft located eight of the fugitives. Two, the little *Askari*, of 590 tons, and the Italian *Pensilvania*, were bombed and shelled in the approaches to Mogadishu. Six more were 'buzzed' at low level and ordered to close the cruiser *Hawkins*. Five were taken in prize, but the sixth, the German *Uckermark* was scuttled. A similar end came to three Italian ships which had not been able to depart Kismayu. Two more vessels were seized when that town was captured on 14 February 1941, along with the decrepit *Durmitor*. African troops entered Mogadishu on 25 February. Of the merchantmen that had fled Italian Somaliland during the campaign, only *Duca degli Abruzzi* and *Somalia* attained the security of Diego Suarez.

Meanwhile *Tannenfels* was over the Saya de Malha Bank between the Seychelles and Mauritius. Here she met the raider *Atlantis* (returning *Durmitor's* prize crew), the *panzerschiff Admiral Scheer*, and the captured vessels *Ketty Brovig* (a Norwegian tanker whose cargo of diesel and fuel oil topped up all the ships present) and *Speybank*. This last was a 5154-ton motor freighter owned by A. Weir & Co of Glasgow. She had been captured by *Atlantis* southwest of India on 31 January 1941, being bound from the Far East to New York with 1500 tons of manganese, 300 tons of rubber, jute, teak, tea, ilmenite and monazite. *Speybank* had been built by Harland & Wolff in 1926, she had a speed of 11 knots and she had taken on enough fuel to undertake the whole voyage without refuelling. Indeed, all the Bank Line ships were typical freighters whose appearance anywhere in the world would excite no suspicion. *Speybank* was just the sort of prize that ought to be sent to Europe. Accordingly *Tannenfels'* First Officer Schneidewind was given a hurried course in Kriegsmarine procedure on board *Atlantis* and was then put in command of *Speybank*. After serving as a raider scouting vessel, she set course for Bordeaux in March 1941, safely discharging her cargo on 11 May 1941. She was preceded by *Tannenfels*, who had arrived on 19 April 1941.

By now, it was becoming evident to the Italian authorities that in spite of the dogged defence of Keren, the British would eventually be pushing through towards Massawa, itself under occasional attack by carrier-borne biplanes. Too close an investment was prevented by minefields in the shallow, reef-strewn approaches to the port. A similar situation existed at Assab, a small Eritrean port just short of Bab el Mandeb.

Experience at Kismayu had shown that escape should not be left to the last minute. Now was a particularly favourable time, as the Royal Navy was fully occupied either chasing all over the Indian Ocean looking for *Atlantis* and *Admiral Scheer*, or escorting convoys in case the raiders found them first. Even if the merchantmen fleeing from Italian ports were sighted, the advantage was not all on the British side. There was still no certain way of identifying a lone ship. A close approach laid the warship open to surprise attack, while long-range expenditure of ammunition earned equal disapproval from the Admiralty. Nor were cruiser captains happy about breaking wireless silence to ask for information regarding a ship which seemed genuine enough. but had happened to make a mistake when replying to a challenge. In addition, many British masters viewed any warship with suspicion and often made off instead of stopping to be identified, thus wasting more of the Royal Navy's time.

In these circumstances it was just possible for Axis merchant ships to escape patrols even in the Bab el Mandeb. A variety of vessels set out from Massawa in February and March 1941. *Wartenfels* could do only five knots, but Kapitän Ahlers took her through declared minefields where there was less chance of interception. Once the only course lay between two British patrol vessels, but neither saw the German freighter which eventually reached Madagascar. The submarines and other warships, such as the sloop *Eritrea* and the disguised AMCs *Ramb I* and *Ramb II*, were expected to make for Bordeaux or Kobe, attacking suitable targets of opportunity en route. They achieved nothing and *Ramb I* (her name stood for *Roma Azienda Monopolio Banane* — Rome Banana Monopoly Company) was sunk by *Leander*. The New Zealand cruiser then co-operated with the Australian *Canberra* in the destruction of *Ketty Brovig* and *Coburg* on 4 March 1941. The latter was a German merchantman which had broken out of Massawa on 20/21 February. Three weeks later, *Leander* followed up these successes by intercepting the Vichy *Charles L.D.* 200 miles off Mauritius.

On 1 March, the 6240-ton *Himalaya* owned by Lloyd Triestino departed Massawa and passed through the Bab el Mandeb. She was the last to do so. *Oder* and *India*, German and Italian ships of 8516 and 6366 tons respectively, made the attempt during the dark moon period on 23 March. *Oder* scuttled herself when stopped by the sloop *Shoreham*. *India* put into Assab, a refuge also sought by *Piave*. *Bertrand Rickmers* left Massawa on 29 March, but survived only until 1 April 1941. The agent of her self-destruction was the destroyer *Kandahar*. *Lichtenfels* did not even get that far, but turned back to Massawa.

All this was in *Himalaya*'s wake as the cargo-liner's diesel hurried her south at 13 knots and round the Cape of Good Hope to reach Rio de Janeiro on 4 April 1941. Four days later, Massawa was overwhelmed, the Axis merchantmen still there being scuttled or captured. The harbour was littered with the wreckage of more than forty ships. Their bottoms blown out, their seacocks smashed, their superstructures gutted, they blocked the entrance and jammed the quay. The 11,760-ton *Colombo* had capsized like an enormous white whale. There was similar destruction at the Dahlak Islands, some forty miles offshore. Five ships had hoped to hide there, slipping away later when the war had moved on. It was a vain hope; the Royal Navy did not overlook them. On 10 June 1941, Assab was captured—and that was the end of the German and Italian ships there.

Then on the night of 24/25 August 1941, British and Indian troops entered Persia from Iraq and the Gulf, while the Soviets invaded from the north. The operation was designed to secure Allied control over the government of the country, prevent Axis infiltration, safeguard oil supplies, and open up a land route between the Indian Ocean to the Soviet Union. It seemed more like piracy as far as the German and Italian merchant seamen, sheltering in neutral Iranian harbours, were concerned.

As a miscellaneous naval force approached Bandar Shahpur, they saw columns of smoke rising into the dawn sky. From the Indian sloop *Lawrence*, from dhows and tugs, boarding parties of bluejackets and soldiers swarmed over the Axis ships. The Australian AMC *Kanimbla* carried men of the Baluchi Regiment, and those not required for shore duty also joined in. The fires were put out and some of the ships saved from sinking. Only the *Weissenfels* was a total loss. *Hohenfels* settled on the bottom, but during subsequent salvage operations, she was pumped out, raised and towed away. Three other Hansa freighters (*Marienfels*, *Sturmfels* and *Wildenfels*) were seized by the British, as were the Italian *Barbara* and *Caboto* (freighters) and *Bronte* (a tanker). Another Italian cargo ship, *Hilda*, was taken two days later at Bandar Abbas.

For the time being the Vichy French port of Djibouti was still being blockaded by the Free French sloops *Savorgnana de Brazza* and *Commandant Duboc*. British help was provided because it was feared that the harbour might become the means of revictualling German raiders at sea and the surviving Italian troops inland. The food shortages in Djibouti became very bad, so the French authorities decided to run cargoes through from Diego Suarez, a distance of 2500 miles. Full-sized merchantmen would be too obvious and too provocative, so it was planned to make the entire voyage in native sailing craft. With walnut-stained faces and wearing turbans, three Frenchmen set out from Madagascar with a local crew. As the 130-ton *Hind* approached Djibouti the Vichy French submarine *Vengeur* launched torpedoes in the general vicinity of the *Savorgnan de Brazza*. Broadcasting a U-boat alarm, the sloop steered for safer waters, thus enabling *Hind* to steal into the harbour and unload 70 tons of food. She was later followed by *Naram Passa*, but five other sailing craft did not make it. On Christmas Eve 1941, the Vichy sloop *d'Iberville* charged through a weak British patrol line signalling 'Stand clear or we open fire.' Thus 300 tons of food were delivered.

Two submarines undertook similar missions and in February 1942, the largest consignment yet (1300 tons) was shipped in in the banana carrier *Bougainville*. Three months later further operations were brought to an end by the British occupation of Madagascar. The ships captured there included *Wartenfels* lying sabotaged and booby-trapped in drydock.

11 The Aftermath of Rheinübung

With the Royal Navy fully engaged in Indian Ocean operations, in the Mediterranean campaigns and in protecting the North Atlantic convoy routes, the middle of 1941 should have been a favourable one for Axis blockade runners. Certainly the German Hgh Command hoped it would be so. Ever since 21 July 1940, they had known of Hitler's definite intention to invade the Soviet Union. Naturally, the instant the troops crossed their start line, Germany's land route from the Far East would be severed, at the very time that huge quantities of raw materials would be required for the 139 divisions scheduled to take part. Although only a few knew the reasons for the build-up which began in August 1940, it was the desire to stockpile as much as possible which indirectly influenced SKL in its insistence that raider captains send captured merchantmen back and not destroy them. It also meant that preparations would have to be made for the transport of Oriental products, especially rubber, by sea. It would not be enough to rely on the occasional arrival of prizes, nor on the comparatively haphazard use of just any merchantman wandering the oceans and combining the roles of supply ship, unarmed scout, prison hulk and blockade runner. The ships would have to be fast, reliable and economical. They would be allocated special routes and they would have to operate to a precise timetable This would enable cargoes to be warehoused in the Far East, prevent accidental interception by U-boats, and enable escort forces to meet them in dangerous areas, particularly the Bay of Biscay; there must be no repetition of the tragic *Tirranna* muddle.

It would be necessary to plan for voyages in both directions. The Japanese were still neutral and required all their merchantmen for their own secret schemes. The Italians, whose economy was linked to their Axis partner's, would help, but even so there were still not enough suitable vessels in the Orient for one-way trips. In any case, the raw materials would have to be purchased with something, so eastward-bound ships would be exporting European goods of value to the Japanese economy. Oberkommando der Kriegsmarine (OKM) began preparations for this regular traffic on 14 November 1940. Bordeaux would be the European terminal of this service, with Tokyo being the headquarters in the Far East, although there would be several points of departure from the Orient. Instructions regarding cargoes would come from the Special Naval Supply Service (MSD) who would also look after the money side of things. Following prewar procedure, MSD would liaise with the Economics Ministry, who would also oversee those private firms tendering for construction and transport contracts abroad. SKL (Operations Division) would make arrangements about routes and escort, and issue orders to the appropriate commands, as well as to the merchantman on passage.

The first complete journey from the Far East to Europe was made by *Ermland*, a Hapag diesel-driven freighter of 6528 tons. Under Kapitän Krage, she sailed from Kobe on 28 December 1940 and met the raider *Orion* at Lamotrek Atoll in the Pacific on 5 January 1941. Some stores were handed over to the warship, the resulting space being cleaned up and fitted out as accommodation for *Orion*'s prisoners. The work was finished within a few hours and *Ermland* departed the same day. Later, *Orion* and her supply oiler *Ole Jacob* caught up, keeping company until 9 January. From then on, the freighter was on her own, rounding Cape Horn and reaching Bordeaux on 4 April 1941. Kapitän Krage had shown that it could be done and orders were sent out for the next three blockade runners to finish loading 11,000 tons of rubber at Dairen, a Manchurian port on the Yellow Sea.

Instructions had already been despatched to all merchantmen in neutral Pacific ports to make for Japan. Some masters had made this move on their own initiative, while others had been designated as supply ships. Seven came from Chile, Mexico, Siam and China to join the thirteen already there after *Ermland's* departure. Not all of them met OKM's requirements, and the number of suitable vessels came down to twelve. It was hoped that this figure would be augmented by the arrival of four prizes.

However, the Far East was not the only source of natural rubber. Another scheme was the despatch of *Karnak*, *Frankfurt* and *Lech* from the Biscay ports (plus *Joao Pessoa* from Vigo) to Brazil, where they would exchange their cargoes for rubber and other South American products. For the purpose of the expedition *Karnak* and *Joao Pessoa* were given the codenames *Hermes* and *Natal*. Quite apart from the industrial contribution these cargoes would make to Germany, the operation was something of a political exercise. It was made under the auspices of the Transport Ministry (Reichsverkehrsministerium) who maintained that they were the only fit people to organize blockade running—with co-operation from the Kriegsmarine. Admiral Dönitz thus had extra cause for annoyance when his U-boats were diverted from 'The Tonnage War' to cover the passage of these particular blockade runners.

Such traffic could not be expected to last very long for on 30 March 1941, the United States government seized all German, Italian and Danish merchantmen in American ports, an action not legally confirmed until 6 June 1941. It could be expected that similar pressure would soon be brought to bear on the Latin American nations, which were also sheltering a number of Italian merchant vessels. They and their compatriots in the central Atlantic islands now received orders from Supermarina to attempt the passage to France, all being routed in a wide sweep west of the Azores. There were a number of interceptions, but for six weeks hardly a day went by without the departure of some Axis merchant-man from a neutral port and the arrival of another in western France.

28 March: The 10,535-ton AGIP tanker *Franco Martelli* left Recife under Capitano Cardillo. In the Bay of Biscay she was the victim of yet another of those chance encounters which seemed to haunt the area. The submarine *Urge* on passage to the Mediterranean sighted her on 18 April. Lieutenant Tomkinson fired his torpedoes and *Franco Martelli* was sunk.

28 March: *Mombaldo* (6213 tons) sailed from Para. She sighted a number of ships but reached Le Verdon via St Jean de Luz on 24 April.

28/29 March: *Frisco* (a 4609-ton tanker) departed Fortaleza in Brazil, arriving St Nazaire on 27 April.

1 April: *Burano*, another tanker—of 4450 tons—departed Tenerife, to deliver 5800 tons of fuel oil at St Nazaire on 21 April.

1 April: The 4722-ton freighter *Capo Alga* also departed Tenerife, her destination being Nantes, arriving on 18 April.

2 April: The German *München* and *Hermonthis* had to be scuttled after being intercepted by the Canadian AMC *Prince Henry*, when they left Callao in Peru as part of Germany's Pacific movements.

21 April: *U106* relieved *U105* off Rio de Janeiro as escort for *Lech*, one of the blockade runners from Europe to Brazil and back again. There was no suggestion that the U-boats should torpedo American ships patrolling the Pan-American Neutrality Zone, but if they performed their usual habit of broadcasting the blockade runner's position, then the submarine would be able to deal with any British warships that were summoned to the scene.

26 April: *Gianna M.* (a 5718-ton tanker) departed Las Palmas.

Ahead of *Gianna M.* was the tanker *Recco*, coming from Tenerife. The morning of 3 May was bright and sunny when the ocean boarding vessel *Hilary* came in sight. *Recco*'s master ordered the scuttling procedure to be set in motion and abandoned ship. *Hilary*'s boarding party stayed in their boat while an officer searched for documents before the tanker foundered. He also found time to open a number of birdcages, releasing canaries, most of whom flew off in hope of reaching land. One was smuggled on board *Hilary* in spite of a ban on pets. The Italians were also recovered, most being prepared to undertake various jobs such as chipping paint during their time in the ship. *Recco* was finished off with gunfire.

The next Saturday was quite different when *Hilary* sighted another tanker which had to be stopped with a shot across her bows at 4 pm on 10 May. It was very rough and Capitano Pozzo ordered the demolition charges to be prepared but the dynamite would not be detonated until the weather moderated and his crew had a chance to abandon ship safely. In the meantime he was given a course to steer, shouted across by one of *Hilary*'s stewards, a former merchant seaman of Italian descent. It was still very rough the next morning, so bad that *Hilary*'s boarding party hoped that they would not be called away. However, the boat was launched, hitting the bottom of the swell, and pulled across to the tanker. Leaving an armed guard on board, the boat returned, bearing a quantity of birdseed for the canary from *Recco* which had been existing on a diet of fig pips. Escorted by the OBV, *Gianna M.* was put into a convoy for Belfast.

29 April: The prize tanker *British Advocate*, captured by *Admiral Scheer* in the Indian Ocean on 20 February, arrived in the Gironde. *Canadolite* was another Bordeaux-arriving prize, this time from the central Atlantic.

5 May: The 6466-ton tanker *Sangro* departed Las Palmas carrying 7560 tons of oil. She only lasted a day. Sighted by Coastal Command, she was successfully taken by the OBV *Camito*, who escorted her prize towards an approaching convoy bound for England. Both ships were sunk by *U97* before 6 May had ended.

That was typical of the to and fro struggles of the Battle of the Atlantic. During the next week nine merchantmen and one AMC were lost as well as *U110*, whose commander, Kapitänleutnant Julius Lemp, had accounted for the liner *Athenia*, the first ship sunk at sea during World War II. *U110* was blown to the surface by depth-charges and rammed on 9 May. Her crew had just enough time to abandon her before she foundered. Kapitänleutnant Lemp was not among the survivors.

That same day, the tanker *Nordmark* (formerly *Westerwald*) was relieved at her South Atlantic fuelling rendezvous by *Egerland*. The 10,845-ton *Nordmark* reached Hamburg—through the English Channel—on 20 May; she had been away from Gotenhafen (Gdynia) since 17/18 September 1940.

Another arrival on 20 May, this time at Bordeaux, was *Dresden*, bringing 202 passengers including 138 Americans from the neutral Egyptian liner *Zamzam*. Originally a Bibby Line ship, *Zamzam* had been sunk in the Atlantic by *Atlantis* on 17 April, because she looked British. *Dresden* was also carrying forty-six guards and prisoners from other vessels destroyed by raiders. She was going to proceed to a neutral port to disembark all the people on board, but instead SKL had ordered *Dresden* to make for France.

One ship that did not reach her destination this month was the Vichy French *Winnepeg* of 8379 tons. She was stopped on 26 May and captured by the Dutch sloop *Van Kinsbergen* east of Martinique.

That was the day after the battleship *Bismarck* had been sunk, the end of Operation Rheinübung into which the Germans had put so much effort—and not just into the movement of the two capital ships. Since the previous autumn, supply ships had been crossing and recrossing the world's oceans; vessels built specially for the Kriegsmarine, whose tanker hulls concealed fuel bunkers, magazines and provision rooms; merchantmen on the run from a neutral port with useful items in their cargoes; captured prizes, whose consignments were of value to some other raider; merchant ships chartered or requisitioned by the Kriegsmarine; vessels whose crews wore Kriegsmarine uniforms or merchant navy clothes or whose masters' and officers' caps bore a shipping company house flag, while the crew sported military headgear. Some supply ships were attached to particular vessels, meeting them at regular intervals. Others drifted in one patch of ocean, servicing every ship that passed by, themselves revictualled regularly by a shuttle service from Europe. Admittedly, the numbers of ships involved were nothing like the British Empire's total, but Royal Navy warships were never very far from safe harbour. The Kriegsmarine had to do everything afloat, directed by occasional, brief signal, for months on end.

Britannia might claim to rule the waves, but it hardly looked like it to any German sailor watching a *panzerschiff* and a disguised raider fuelling from a big tanker, with a U-boat alongside and a couple of prizes and a blockade runner hove-to in the background, their boats pulling leisurely across the sunlit sea with captured cigarettes and eggs and secret documents.

But even this supply organization was not enough for Operation Rheinübung, the set-piece justification for Grossadmiral Raeder's balanced battlefleet. Before *Bismarck* and *Prinz Eugen* could proceed, a whole range of weather ships, supply vessels, tankers and scouts had to be deployed for the benefit of the two big ships themselves (the *Admiral Hipper*-class cruisers were notoriously heavy on fuel) and for the associated raider and U-boat dispositions. The problem of fuelling the last-mentioned would soon become urgent as in July 1941 British diplomatic pressure eventually forced Spain to stop German tankers anchoring in the Canaries. This virtually coincided with Portugal's permission that British oilers could make similar use of the Azores.

After *Bismarck* had been sunk, the British Admiralty could confidently assume that the Germans had made prior arrangements for refuelling at sea. Indeed, some officers with worldwide navigational experience knew where suitable areas of calm seas existed. Confirmation seemed to come from infrequent bearings on unidentifiable signals. However, warships could rarely be despatched to investigate mere guesswork, and when they were, whoever had been transmitting, was gone. But in May 1941, Admiralty intelligence had gained possession of something that took a lot of guesswork out of one aspect of the sea war.

Contrary to what SKL thought and her own crew believed, *U110* had not sunk immediately on 9 May. She had stayed afloat and under tow for almost two days. During that time an Enigma-type ciphering machine and codebooks had been removed. Already some information was being gleaned from items captured on board the trawler *Krebs* and the weather ship *München*. Now the Admiralty could read signals to U-boats. This was not only of benefit in rerouteing convoys to avoid wolf-packs, although some British signals were being intercepted by the Germans resulting in move and counter-move. Admittedly the Admiralty still could not decipher messages to raiders or blockade runners, but if a U-boat were ordered to meet a supply ship, the Royal Navy could be there too. If U-boats were told to watch out for a raider passing along a certain route, the Admiralty would know of that as well. And if a couple of U-boats were instructed to escort a blockade runner through a particular area, it could be a sentence of death for that merchantman.

The acquisition of this secret advantage did not hold good without interruption for the rest of the war. The Germans changed their ciphers from time to time, which meant a delay while the new codes were decrypted. The Admiralty's knowledge did not always guarantee success. There were not always enough warships or aircraft to follow up even certain information. Sometimes the German vessels failed to put in appearance for reasons of their own. And when battle was joined, the outcome depended, as ever, on the quality of men and ships.

But in May, June and July 1941, the German naval supply network was dealt a series of blows from which it never recovered. Most ships were sunk by a combination of scuttling and gunfire. The latter was employed to discourage scuttling, either in the form of frightening nearmisses or by destroying the bridge and thus preventing the scuttling order from being given. If this had already been done, then the derelict was destroyed as a danger to navigation, to prevent her being boarded and salved by a lurking U-boat, and to provide useful target practice for the gunners. Some vessels were captured, each seizure contributing something more to the knowledge about the enemy's signals and the location of fuelling rendezvous—although this took time to be analyzed and was not of immediate significance in the great round-up of mid-1941. Many Germans believed that their interception was the result of earlier successes, or was due to lax security, most likely on the part of the Italians. They never suspected their own communications.

An additional factor in the British success was that the sudden increase in naval activity from Greenland to the South Atlantic, coincidentally encountered a number of vessels which had nothing to do with Rheinübung. First to go was *Lech*, homeward-bound from Rio de Janeiro. On 28 May, after her submarine escort had been ordered to leave her, the blockade runner was intercepted and had to be scuttled. Next day, two German weather ships were lost.

And then in June 1941, it seemed that almost every day tolled the end of yet another Axis ship.

18. *HMS Truant* which intercepted *Tropic Sea* in the Bay of Biscay in September 1940. Forty British prisoners were rescued and the Germans were forced to scuttle their prize.

19. The Norwegian *Tirranna* was captured by the raider *Atlantis* in 1940. Under prize crew she arrived safely off the Gironde, but had to wait while the shore authorities made arrangements for her to proceed upriver. On 22 September she was sunk by the British submarine *Tuna*, with heavy loss of life.

20. *Pelagos*, one of the three factory ships and eleven whalecatchers taken in prize in the Antarctic by the aptly named *Pinguin*. One catcher was retained as an auxiliary and two more were intercepted in the Atlantic. All the rest reached France by March 1941.

21. Hamburg-Amerika's *Ermland* was the first blockade runner from Japan to Bordeaux in December 1940—April 1941. Renamed *Weserland* she went out to Japan again, but was lost on the return voyage in January 1944.

22. The tanker *Friedrich Breme* was a supply ship, not a blockade runner, but this scene on board *HMS Sheffield* is typical of those after any Axis merchantman had been sunk. Here the German master is allowed to sit in on the interrogation of his crew.

23. Hamburg-Südamerika's *Rio Grande* in her peacetime colours. During the war she voyaged from Brazil to France, did a round trip to Japan and back, returned to Japan, and commenced an abortive run but had to turn back in the Indian Ocean. She was eventually intercepted in January 1944.

24. The US cruiser *Omaha* closing the German blockade runner *Odenwald* in the South Atlantic on 6 November 1941.

25. Every little helps; short of fuel, the destroyer *Somers* rigged a sail to assist fuel economy while escorting *Odenwald* to Trinidad.

26. *Elsa Essberger*, seen here in ballast prewar, put into the neutral Spanish port of El Ferrol on her homeward run in January 1942.

27. The British cruiser *Dunedin* captured four ships and forced another to scuttle during her career. She is seen here at Freetown in 1940. The seaplane carrier *Pegasus* is in the background.

28. This photograph of *Cortellazzo* was taken when Italy was still neutral.

29. From the US cruiser *Savannah* Rear-Admiral Read signalled the destroyer *Eberle*: 'YEAST FROM CACTUS. NEVER MIND DUTCH FLAG. PILE IN THERE. THIS IS A RUNNER.' Thus was *Karin* intercepted on 10 March 1943.

30. *Pietro Orseolo* was named after a Doge of Venice. She did a round trip from Japan to Bordeaux and back again. On her final home run she was torpedoed in the Bay of Biscay by the US submarine *Shad*, but docked with most of her cargo intact on 2 April 1943.

31. Hamburg-Amerika's *Osorno* was the only surface blockade runner to reach France in the winter of 1943–4.

32. A US Navy Consolidated PB4Y Liberator crosses the Cornish coast on a Biscay control.

33. The last blockade runner: *U532* at Liverpool in May 1945. A cylindrical container of rubber is being unloaded from the free-flooding casing. Ingots of tin are stacked on the foredeck.

3 June: *Belchen*, a tanker refuelling U-boats in the Davis Strait, was sunk by the cruisers *Aurora* and *Kenya*.

4 June: The tanker *Gedania*, which earlier in the war had delivered a cargo of whale-oil to Occupied Europe, was captured by the OBV *Marsdale* in mid-Atlantic.

4 June: *Gonzenheim*, a supply-cum-patrol ship, was sighted by a Swordfish from the carrier *Victorious* north of the Azores. The AMC *Esperance Bay* could not catch her, but the battleship *Nelson* and the cruiser *Neptune* prevented her escape. *Gonzenheim* sunk.

4 June: *Esso Hamburg*, a tanker, was located by the cruiser *London* and the destroyer *Brilliant* just north of the Equator. *Esso Hamburg* sunk.

5 June: The tanker *Egerland* was sunk by *London* and *Brilliant*.

6 June: Kapitän Vagt's *Elbe*, a 9179-ton blockade runner belonging to NDL was sighted and sunk by Swordfish from the carrier *Eagle* near the Azores. With her went the cargo of rubber which had been loaded at Dairen on 20 April. The present situation was obviously too dangerous for blockade runners to attempt the passage through the Atlantic. It was too late to halt *Regensburg*. She had left Dairen on 5 May, but *Ramses* had not sailed until a week later. SKL therefore ordered Kapitän Falcke to take his freighter back to Japan, which he did.

12 June: The tanker *Friedrich Breme*, was sighted by *Sheffield* in mid-Atlantic. She attempted to escape and was sunk after she had begun her scuttling procedure.

15th June: The cruiser *Dunedin* captured *Lothringen* in the central Atlantic after the tanker had been found by *Eagle's* aircraft.

17 June: The AMC *Pretoria Castle* captured the Vichy *Desirade* east of the Antilles.

18 June: *U138* was sunk west of Gibraltar by destroyers of Force H, out searching for supply ships.

21 June: The supply ship *Babitonga* was intercepted by *London* near the Equator. *Babitonga* scuttled herself.

23 June: Force H destroyers and *Marsdale* found the supply ship *Alstertor* after she had been sighted the previous day west of Gibraltar. *Alstertor* sunk.

28 June: The weather-reporting trawler *Lauenburg* was captured by the destroyer *Tartar* near Jan Mayen.

29 June: The Italian blockade runner *Ernani*, coming from Las Palmas, was torpedoed by mistake by *U103*.

30 June: *Dunedin* captured the Vichy French merchantman *Ville de Tamatave* in the South Atlantic.

Of course, the oceans are very wide and there were still gaps in the Royal Navy's coverage. The technique of fuelling at sea was being continually practised and improved, but ships still had to return to port from time to time. It was at such periods that *Kota Pinang*, *Ermland* and *Spichern* returned from their Rheinübung duties. The Italian vessels *Atlanta*, *Todaro*, *Butterfly* and *XXIV Maggio* reached France from the Canaries and South America. Most importantly, Kapitän Harder's *Regensburg* arrived at Bordeaux on 27 June with a valuable cargo of rubber.

Early July 1941 was the time scheduled for *Karnak*, *Frankfurt* and *Joao Pessao* to bring their Brazilian cargoes back to Bordeaux. Three Italian vessels would be making a breakout at the same time, while other ships in South America were also ordered to move. The operation would obviously stir up a great deal of British activity, so those disguised raiders that were still at sea were ordered to keep well clear of the area.

Some ships did get through. *Benno*, formerly the captured tanker *Ole Jacob* was one, reaching Bordeaux on 19 July with her tanks empty after supplying the raider *Orion*. But for the most part July was a repeat of June's catalogue of disasters. *Joao Pessoa* was the only one of the Transport Ministry's ships to make the return from Brazil. (It was hoped that she could make a similar journey the following year, but she ran aground and was wrecked near San Sebastian on 8 June 1942.) *Frankfurt* was lost while the 7209-ton *Karnak* was intercepted by the AMC *Canton* on 10 July. She then scuttled herself northwest of St Paul in the South Atlantic. In the same area, *Dunedin* captured the Vichy *Ville de Rouen* on 22 July.

Three days later time ran out for *Erlangen*, continuing her eventful voyage from New Zealand and the South Pacific via Chile and Cape Horn. She was southeast of the River Plate when the cruiser *Newcastle* came in sight. The crew opened the seacocks and abandoned her, pulling across towards the British warship. Suddenly an oerlikon opened fire on them, injuring two men in the nearest boat, one of them being shot in the bottom. The firing stopped abruptly. Apparently an officer had seized the gun, although it was never clear whether this was some sort of personal animosity or whether he had decided that he ought to implement the Admiralty's instructions about forcibly preventing survivors from scuttling and leaving their ship. Whatever his reasons, they were not known to the leading seaman who knocked him from the gun. The Germans were brought on board and accommodated in the canteen. Meanwhile a damage control team had been put on board *Erlangen*. After several hours' work they still could not halt the flooding and they were recalled, permitting *Erlangen* to founder. During the passage to Freetown, it was learned that the boarding party had recovered quite a number of items from the sinking ship, it being reasonably assumed that the Germans had left them behind because they had no further use for them. Under the rules of prize warfare, anything that did not belong to the prize court was personal property and sacrosanct. Accordingly, it was ordered that all the liberated items should be handed in and given back to the Germans before they were sent off to the prison camp—to the obvious delight and disappointment of the respective parties.

On 14 August the AMC *Circassia* captured the Italian *Stella* coming from Recife. Next day another ship was scuttled northeast of the Amazon, being intercepted by the cruiser *Despatch* and the AMC *Pretoria Castle*. The 3667-ton *Nordeney* was the last Axis merchantman to attempt to reach home from a port in the Americas. There might still be occasional supply ships or captured prizes at sea, but from now on the only Axis merchant ships on ocean passage would be blockade runners to and from the Far East. Just completing their voyages from Brazil were *Africana* and *Himalaya*, entering Bordeaux with an escort of M-boote. The latter, under Capitano Sambo, with a crew of twenty-seven was delivering a cargo of 3417 tons consisting of skins, fats, oils, vegetable products, minerals, wool, ipecacuana and horsehair.

12 The Blockade Runners' Heyday

Germany's invasion of the Soviet Union immediately cut the Trans-Siberian route from the Far East. The only way natural rubber, certain strategic ores and important edible oils could now reach Occupied Europe was by sea. Yet the invasion had also opened a new convoy route for the Royal Navy to defend, just at a time when severe losses were being suffered in the Mediterranean. Although co-operative, the United States Navy was still officially neutral, but soon the American, British and Dutch fleets were reeling under more heavy blows in the Orient. So, for almost a year in 1941 and 1942, German and Italian blockade runners passed to and fro practically unmolested, bringing 75,000 tons of products to Europe and delivering 32,540 tons of equipment and chemicals to Japan.

Once on their voyage to Europe across the Pacific and around Cape Horn, the blockade runners maintained radio silence, passing rearranged points at specific times. When one was due, U-boats and aircraft were not allowed to attack any merchantmen in a 200-mile wide lane in mid-Atlantic northeastwards from the latitude of the Canaries, keeping to the east of the Azores and then heading due east into Bordeaux. Local escort was provided through the Biscay approaches, with mid-ocean cover sometimes being provided by U-boats.

Cargoes were unloaded at Custom House Quay, Bordeaux, and then the ship was refitted before the next voyage. Machinery was inspected, and parts replaced. Armament was installed, decks strengthened and magazine accommodation provided, plus quarters for the extra crew and passengers being carried. At least four scuttling charges, each weighing as much as 75 kg were secreted in the bottom of the ship. These were armed ready for use as soon as the ship put to sea. When their 7–9 minute fuzes ran out, the effect would be the same as four 35.5-cm (14-inch) shells hitting the vessel simultaneously. The crew usually kept all their personal gear packed ready for abandoning ship.

After being drydocked to have her bottom cleaned of marine growth which cut speed and blocked inlets, the ship went back alongside the dockyard wharf for final adjustments. Then came sea trials and loading at Bassens North or perhaps proceeding to another Biscay port for some particular consignment. At last the blockade runner would be waiting in the Gironde for her mine-sweeping escort and sailing orders.

It was, as the following list shows, a timetable of sailings as frequent as any peacetime service, with supply ships and prizes being slotted into the programme.

20 June 1941: *Anneliese Essberger* (John T. Essberger; freighter; 5173 tons; Kapitän Prahm) departed Dairen.

21 August: *Odenwald* (HAPAG freighter; 5098 tons; Kapitän Loehrs) departed Yokohama.

August–September: *Benno* (ex-prize tanker *Ole Jacob;* 8306 tons; Kapitän Steinkrauss) departed Bordeaux.

10 September: *Anneliese Essberger* arrived Bordeaux.

21 September: *Rio Grande* (Hamburg-Südamerika freighter; 6062 tons; Kapitän von Allwörden) departed Bordeaux.

21 September: *Burgenland* (HAPAG freighter; 7320 tons; Kapitän Schladebach) departed Kobe.

24 September: *Kota Nopan* (prize; 7322 tons) departed South Pacific.

27 September: *Silvaplane* (prize: 4793 tons) departed South Pacific.

September: *Kota Pinang* (U-boat supply ship; 7275 tons) departed France.

October: *Benno* arrived and departed Kobe.

14 October: *Elsa Essberger* (John T. Essberger freighter; 6104 tons; Kapitän Bahl) departed Sasebo.

October: *Portland* (HAPAG freighter; 7132 tons; Kapitän Piunnecke) departed Bordeaux.

21 October: *Spreewald* (HAPAG freighter; 5083 tons; Kapitän Bull) departed Dairen.

October: *Python* (U-boat supply ship; 3664 tons; Kapitän Lueders) departed Europe.

15 November: *Cortellazzo* (Oriens di Trieste/Lloyd Triestino freighter; 5292 tons; Capitano Mancusi) departed Dairen.

17 November: *Kota Nopan* and *Silvaplana* arrived Bordeaux.

2 December: *Pietro Orseolo* (Sidarma de Fiume freighter; 6344 tons; Capitano Zustovich) departed Kobe.

6 December: *Rio Grande* arrived Osaka.

10 December: *Burgenland* arrived Bordeaux.

24 December: *Osorno* (HAPAG freighter; 6951 tons; Kapitän Hellmann) departed Kobe.

1 January 1942: *Portland* arrived Osaka.

15 January: *Elsa Essberger* arrived El Ferrol.

25 January: *Doggerbank* (ex-prize *Speybank;* Hansa freighter; 8998 tons; Kapitän Schneidewind) departed Bordeaux.

28 January: *Cortellazzo* arrived Bordeaux.

31 January: *Rio Grande* departed Kobe.

7 February: *Fusijama* (Oriens di Trieste/Lloyd Triestino frieghter; 6244 tons; Capitano Ghe) departed Kobe.

18 February: *Münsterland* (HAPAG freighter; 6408 tons; Kapitän Uebel) departed Yokohama.

19 February: *Osorne* arrived Bordeaux.

24 February: *Pietro Orseolo* arrived Bordeaux.

26 February: *Portland* departed Yokohama.

March: *Tannenfels* (Hansa freighter; 7840 tons; Kapitän Haase) departed Bordeaux.

7 March: *Germania* (tanker; 9851 tons) departed Bordeaux.

16 April: *Dresden* (NDL freighter; 5567 tons; Kapitän Jäger) departed Bordeaux.

16 April: *Rio Grande* arrived Bordeaux.

26 April: *Fusijama* arrived Bordeaux.

10 May: *Portland* arrived Bordeaux.

12 May: *Tannenfels* arrived Yokohama.

May: *Regensburg* (NDL freighter; 8068 tons; Kapitän Harder) departed Bordeaux.

17 May: *Münsterland* arrived Bordeaux.

7 July: *Regensburg* arrived Yokohama.

The supply ships followed Der Prisenweg (The Prize Route) until it was convenient for them to break off and proceed towards their designated rendezvous areas. *Doggerbank* was another virtually independent command. She had been adapted as a disguised minelayer as well as an armed supply ship. The conversion was undertaken by Kriegsmarine-Werft at Bordeaux, although the mines were loaded at La Pallice. Officially designated HS (*Hilfschiff*) 53, the work was done in such a way that she could easily revert to a blockade running merchant vessel. Indeed, most of her crew were merchant seamen, under the command of reservist Oberleutnant zur See Schneidewind, formerly *Tannenfels'* First Officer. *Doggerbank* laid her mines off South Africa, bluffed her way past an Anson aircraft, a cruiser, and an AMC. She then served as a supply ship in the South Atlantic. Eventually she proceeded to Djakarta and Yokohama, where she disembarked the raider *Michel*'s prisoners on 19 August 1942.

The prizes *Kota Nopan* and *Silvaplana* were the respective captures of *Komet* and *Atlantis*. *Kota Nopan* was carrying rubber, tin and manganese. Rubber (2100 tons of it) also featured in *Silvaplana*'s cargo, together with wax, vanilla, teak, 45 tons of coffee, 500 tons of tin, and 50 cases of Balinese souvenir idols. It is not clear what employment they found in Germany's war economy.

The Italian ships were usually requisitioned by the Italian government— (there was talk of converting them as AMCs)—their masters either being temporarily commissioned into the Regia Navale, or being assigned a naval officer as supernumerary commander. To all intents and purposes, however, they were merchant ships. *Pietro Orseolo*'s cargo was divided into German and Italian consignments. It included 1988 tons of rubber and 4486 tons of edible oils for Germany with 83 tons of tin, 28 tons of tyres and 21 tons of wood oil for Italy.

The tankers were the most efficient for the bulk transport of edible oils. They could also serve as supply oilers on the outward passage, while finding room in their dry-cargo space for at least a few tons of rubber. *Germania* did not get very far, however, as she had to turn back in the Bay of Biscay.

It was against orders to keep going after being sighted by aircraft during the outward journey, nevertheless Kapitän Haase decided to take a chance after his *Tannenfels* was spotted by Coastal Command. He was rewarded for his audacity by proceeding without interception, but out in the Atlantic No. 2 Hold caught fire. Explosions were blowing drums of chemicals into the air as the first and second officers donned gasmasks and clambered down into the hold to get at the seat of the fire. Meanwhile another team was manhandling hot containers up onto the deck and throwing them over the side. The blaze was extinguished just before it reached a hundred drums of ether-chloroform. Recovering from that experience, *Tannenfels* ran into a hurricane in the South Atlantic which damaged her superstructure, but she delivered the rest of her cargo of chemicals, tractors and machine-tools.

It was customary for blockade runners to be escorted by one or two U-boats for part of their journey, a practice opposed by Admiral Dönitz, not only because it was a distraction from The Tonnage War, but because of its tactical impracticability. The idea was that if a British warship appeared, the U-boat would dive and torpedo the enemy. However, the submarine would have to keep close to the merchantman, and once dived would take a long time to get into an attacking position, while the cruiser kept well clear and opened fire at long range. There was also the possibility of a tragic mistake if the blockade runner arrived so early or late that she was outside the prohibitive period. Admiral Dönitz had no way of knowing that since the capture of *U110* the U-boats carried their own contagion of disaster with them.

At various times British Intelligence was able to decipher rendezvous positions broadcast by Befehlshaber der Unterseeboote (C-in-C U-boats or BdU). Thus, after *Kota Pinang*'s departure from Bordeaux had been reported, the cruisers *Sheffield* and *Kenya* were ordered to look out for her. *Kenya*'s Walrus found her north of the Azores on an evening of low cloud. The cruiser was directed towards the supply ship and on 3 October 1941, *Kota Pinang* was hit by 6-inch (15.2-cm) shells, blew up and sank.

In the South Atlantic, U-boats exercised an even more baleful influence on German surface operations, sometimes by mere chance and sometimes through the Admiralty reading of their instructions. In the early dark hours of 4 November 1941, the Admiralty oiler *Olwen*, proceeding independently between Brazil and Freetown, reported being shelled by some unseen assailant, apparently a surface warship of some sort. Immediately the Royal Navy despatched *Dorsetshire*, *Dunedin*, *Canton*, *Koningen Emma* and *Prinses Beatrix* to hunt down and destroy this raider. At the same time Rear-Admiral Jonas H. Ingram of the United States Navy was informed as this action had taken place in the Pan-American Neutrality Zone which now extended to 20° West.

The American authorities had long considered the possibility of the expansion of German influence through Vichy-held West Africa, across the islands of the South Atlantic and into the South American republics. They were determined to prevent this and were already forestalling any Nazi advance by the construction of commercial airfields which in wartime could be used by US military aircraft. These overseas expeditions were escorted by Task Force 3, comprising the old cruisers *Memphis*, *Milwaukee*, *Cincinnati* and *Omaha* with the modern destroyers *Somers*, *Winslow*, *Moffett*, *Davis* and *Jouett*. These ships also patrolled the Pan-American Neutrality Zone off Brazil, and, like warships in the North Atlantic, were darkened and ready for action just as if the United States were already at war.

Their commander, Rear-Admiral Ingram, was a big man, a colourful and forceful personality, yet also a man of tact. In 1941, he was fifty-five, having commanded a destroyer, a cruiser and a battleship. He had been the US Navy's public relations officer and a notable football player and coach. Admiral Ingram was a 'shirt-sleeve diplomat.' Ashore, he established such a close friendship with President Vargas and the Brazilian people that the US Navy could do no wrong. Whatever facilities were requested were granted. He set up a farm outside Recife to supply all the task force's meat and vegetables without calling upon US logistics. He so endeared himself to Brazilian naval ratings that when he left at the end of the war, they presented him with a nugget of Brazilian gold so that he could always take with him a piece of Brazil. Afloat, Admiral Ingram inspired and trained his men so that, in spite of their idyllic surroundings they were as eager and prepared for battle as any unit in harsher conditions.

This was the force co-operating with the Royal Navy in the search for the raider that had fired on *Olwen*. It is not clear what they would do if they did find the raider, but if he wanted a fight then he would get it. However, the Americans saw nothing until 6 November, when *Omaha* and *Somers* were returning to Recife 657 miles away. It was still virtually dark as they approached the Equator sighting a distant merchant ship. She was heading north without lights, and Task Group 3.6 steered to investigate what could well be the disguised raider. In the growing light her answering flags spelled out *Willmoto*. Her name and port of registry (Philadelphia) could be seen on her stern under the Stars and Stripes. Yet there was something suspicious about her. Captain T.E. Chandler of *Omaha* ordered her to stop and sent away a boarding party armed with Thompson submachine-guns under Lieutenant G.K. Carmichael.

At once *Willmoto* signalled 'Am sinking. Send boats' and began abandoning ship. Ignoring the survivors, the boarding party heard two muffled explosions below decks, but they clambered aboard in a haze of smoke which was coming from the hold. However, there was no fire; it was only fumes from the explosions. The damage was not severe and it was dealt with promptly. Seacocks were closed and manhole covers replaced, the securing bolts having been left alongside. A couple of men also examined the hull from outside, in spite of the interest taken by sharks in their activity. Meanwhile the boarders had learned that this vessel was in fact the German *Odenwald*, running the British blockade with 3800 tons of raw rubber. Kapitän Loehrs had not been ordered to scuttle in the event of an American interception. When he eventually realized his ship was going to be seized, the process had had to be hurried, which was why it had not been effective.

The resulting damage provided a good enough reason for escorting *Odenwald* to Port of Spain in Trinidad. The boarding party and ships' companies later shared the salvage money paid out for saving her, although judgement was not finally made until 1947.

But what justification could there be for later taking the freighter to San Juan in Puerto Rico where she arrived on 17 November 1941? Indeed, what legal justification was there for stopping a merchant vessel of a theoretically friendly power in the first place. She was inside the Pan-American Neutrality Zone, but on the high seas outside the legal three-mile limit. However, back in 1819, the United States government had passed a law forbidding the import of negro slaves, although slavery itself was not abolished until the American Civil War. That law gave the US Navy the right to stop and seize any ship suspected of carrying slaves or of being engaged in the slave trade. That law, argued Rear-Admiral Ingram and Captain Chandler, gave the *USS Omaha* the right to stop and seize the German *MV Odenwald*. The German government protested when *Odenwald* and her rubber stayed in American custody—but in the last weeks of 1941 there were lots of things to protest about.

Nobody ever did find the raider that had shelled *Olwen*—without doing any damage. It was in fact a surfaced U-boat. Her commander's gunfire had indirectly been the cause of *Odenwald*'s seizure. An even more direct cause of loss was the Admiralty's interception of signals to U-boats regardng rendezvous with the raider *Atlantis*. After she was sunk by the cruiser *Devonshire*, similar intelligence led to the destruction of the supply ship *Python* on 1 December 1941. Even more unfortunate was *Spreewald*. She was in the North Atlantic when identified by Kapitänleutnant Cremer in *U333* as a Blue Funnel liner. *Spreewald* was sunk by German torpedoes on 31 January 1942.

Of course U-boats could provide no protection against air attack which was a growing threat in the Bay of Biscay. In March 1941, the RAF, previously restricted to preannounced danger zones, was given permission to attack hostile merchantmen wherever they were found and at any time outside neutral territorial waters. To avoid mistakes the aircrew were given a limit much greater than the three miles usually designated for territorial waters. Similar permission and instructions had already been given to Royal Navy warships; indeed, whole areas were prohibited zones where even neutral merchantmen entered at their own peril. However, there were often various operational reasons why an all-out offensive could not be launched immediately an area was declared a 'sink at sight' zone. There might not be enough ships to cover the area, or the aircraft could not carry a worthwhile bombload.

Thus, although Coastal Command extended its patrols right across the Bay of Biscay in August 1941, it was not until December of that year that they achieved a significant success against the blockade runners who were known to be using the Iberian coastal route along with small vessels bringing cargoes from Spain and Portugal—navigational hazards sometimes force ships farther out to sea than the three-mile limit.

On 23 December 1941, a Sunderland from No. 10 RAAF Squadron sighted a large tanker 220 miles northwest of Cape Finisterre. No such Allied vessel was expected in the area, so she was deemed to be hostile. Not having anything else on board, the flying boat dropped its anti-submarine depth-charges. The tanker was damaged but maintained her course and a British destroyer was sent to overhaul her. On the other side an escort of U-boats and aircraft was being prepared. Next day another Sunderland appeared from the same squadron guiding in a Bristol Beaufort of No. 22 Squadron, which arrived when the tanker was a few hundred yards off the Spanish coast. The Beaufort's torpedo did not miss. The tanker was mortally injured and was only saved from sinking by being beached at Carino. So ended *Benno*. Once again Kapitän Steinkrauss had finished a voyage on the Spanish coast.

This was the only success that British forces could claim against blockade runners during this period. Because it had occurred within Spanish territorial waters, Coastal Command had to wait three months before the fuss died down and they were again able to attack all merchantmen within 20 miles—and all identified Germans within five miles—of the Spanish coast. During that time *Elsa Essberger* moved round from El Ferrol to Bordeaux, delivering 4325 tons of rubber, 1512 tons of foodstuffs and edible oils, 858 tons of resin, tallow, leather, duck feathers, black bristles and ores, 65 tons of dried egg yolk and 7½ tons of nutmeg.

Axis blockade runners seemed so expert at getting through that it was wondered whether British ships could raid Harstad in the guise of German merchantmen in the winter of 1941–2. The former Q-ships *Cape Sable* and *City of Durban* embarked British and Norwegian Commandos to destroy a fish oil factory and Axis-controlled shipping. They sailed from Sullom Vöe, but the operation was called off after a meteorological Heinkel He111 sighted the two ships and obviously regarded them as suspicious. The appearance and subsequent disappearance of this mysterious force seems to have caused some confusion at German headquarters.

This blockade running period which had proved so rewarding for the Axis had also marked the loss of one of the most successful interceptors of blockade runners, 'Dancing' *Dunedin*. On 24 November 1941, the cruiser was on patrol 240 miles northeast of St Paul's Rocks when she was sighted by *U124*. For forty minutes as the U-boat porpoised to and from the surface with a rope jammed around the diving planes, Kapitänleutnant Möhr set up his attack on the zig-zagging target. Then *Dunedin* suddenly turned onto a completely different course. Without much hope of hitting, the German fired three torpedoes at very long range. After five minutes twenty-three seconds, there were two explosions. *Dunedin* rolled onto her beam ends, then over the other way, righted herself and sank stern first. The sun was hot. The sea was sparkling—and alive with sharks and barracuda.

Able Seaman David Fraser narrowly escaped death as he helped a drowning man, who died just as he reached him. Sergeant Harry King supported a badly wounded Marine for forty-eight hours. They and others were later commended for their fortitude and care when, in the words of the official citation, 'the patience of others was wearing a little thin due to the hardship all were suffering' (ADM1/12272: *HMS Dunedin*).

There are in this book many references to ships being sunk and survivors being picked up. That searing experience and the emotions felt by rescued and rescuers were common to all nationalities. Let this letter speak for them all. It was written to Admiral Hodges at Trinidad from the captain of the Lykes Brothers' ship which found all that was left of *Dunedin*'s complement of nearly five hundred men.

I herewith acknowledge receipt of your very kind letter with reference to the Survivors from H.M.S. Dunedin, and humble apologize for not being able to send acknowledgment at once, as there was no Boat. The Survivors? When I stood on my deck and looked down at them on the Tender, all smiling and happy except for their injuries, and I believe restored to good health, and picture the scene when we took them out of the water 10 day's before. 72 of them, some unconscious Delirious and hysterics badly lacerated with all kinds of wounds, as we spread them out on the hatch examined and treated them as best we could, Then moved them in to the Officers and crews Bunk to the extent that was possible, What a task;

So many was close, Close to the Borderline. The little pencilled notes from individuals that found its way to me after they had left was very touching.

And to see them all so happy when left us is very much of a reward, all any one could wish.

A few of these men fortunately came to us very little the worce for wear, and these was very help full to us, There was E.T.H. Lavington Ch. Yeom. and very outstanding in their good work was R.D. Butler P.O.P/JX127105, what a Man, and A.H. Hicks Eng. Room Artf. X.941 E.B. These men were outstanding in their usefullness and unceasing attention to their more unfortunet ship mate, workink with us from early morning to late in to the night, They should be much appreciated, and was by us.

I am very sincerely Yours
O.H. Olsen
Master S.S. Nishmaha.

13 Difficult Days

On 21 March 1942, Lord Selborne, the new Minister of Economic Warfare, addressed a memorandum to the British Cabinet. It assumed that the resources of Occupied Europe were sufficient for the military requirements of Germany and Italy, with the exception of rubber, wolfram and tin. Improvisation in the manufacture and use of goods employing these substances meant that only very small quantities of these natural raw materials would be needed to maintain the standard of artificial products. Perhaps as few as a dozen cargoes a year would be sufficient (and, in fact, the Germans had done so well that they were able to export artificial rubber to Sweden during the middle of the war). Japan, however, had gained access to these resources and needed small numbers of ball bearings, instruments and machine-tools. Equal priority must be given to intercepting blockade runners in both directions. Sinking outward-bound ships would not only injure Japan's industry and German finance, but would be the most effective way of preventing these vessels from ever returning again.

In May, June and July 1942, Lord Selborne reiterated his arguments while the Japanese rampaged through the Far East, while German panzers swept through the Soviet Union and North Africa, while Malta seemed about to fall, and while convoy PQ17 and the Czech village of Lidice were destroyed. The various authorities considered these memoranda, especially the suggestion that a strike on Bordeaux would severely dislocate the European terminus of the service. The navy could not send surface warships 500 miles from Plymouth, through all the Biscay patrols and then 62 miles up the Gironde past all the shore defences and batteries. Submarines could not now operate close inshore; minefields, trawlers and aircraft made that too hazardous. The Royal Marines said that three Army divisions would be required if an expedition had to fight its way up the estuary, securing the banks as it went.

The Foreign Office did not want area bombing of the third largest port in France; that would cause too many civilian casualties with adverse effect on

French opinion. The RAF could not guarantee precision attacks on individual vessels in a crowded port ringed with AA guns. However, the RAF had begun minelaying in the Gironde estuary, while the Royal Navy had established submarine patrols farther out in the Bay of Biscay. Both services preferred interception at sea, but they could not be everywhere at once, attacking U-boats, defending convoys, participating in combined operations and looking for a fast blockade runner which might turn out to be an old empty vessel being moved round the coast to serve as an accommodation ship. It would help if they could have better advance notice of German activity—and that was what the RAF was starting to provide.

A period of fine weather during the summer of 1942 enabled reconnaissance aircraft to photograph all the ports of Europe within a few days. The Shipping Movements Section at RAF Medmenham's Central Interpretation Unit then made a comprehensive card-index of stereoscopic photographs covering all German-controlled merchantmen over 2500 tons. Subsequent pictures were compared with this index and new construction identified. It soon became apparent which ones were potential blockade runners and how they fitted into the docking and loading schedules. Vertical and oblique photographs of these particular units were used to prepare recognition silhouettes for aircrew. When runners were expected to sail, Bordeaux was given twice-weekly and then daily coverage. The section was not infallible. It could not always be certain that apparently empty ships were only decoy movements in the Gironde estuary.

Meanwhile, taking advantage of the longer night hours as the North Atlantic winter approached, the German sailings began again. Ever since the early days of the war, the 7744-ton tanker *Charlotte Schliemann* had been at Las Palmas, remaining there after Allied pressure had ended her U-boat fuelling activities in 1941. Now, in August 1942, Kapitän Röthe was ordered to the Far East, supplying raiders and U-boats in the South Atlantic and Indian Ocean en route. When her duties in the Orient had been completed she would return with her tanks full of edible oils. Two more tankers, both Kriegsmarine vessels, were also despatched, *Uckermark* and her near-sister, the steam-turbine *Ermland*, both of 10,698 tons. It could not be said that *Uckermark* had had an altogether happy career so far—she had started life as the notorious *Altmark*.

Because of the increase in aerial activity, Kapitän von Zatorski's *Uckermark* was given an escort of three torpedo boats through the Bay of Biscay. However, after the little force had sailed on 9 August it was sighted by a British aircraft. Accordingly it was decided to return to France. A similar out-and-back trip was performed by *Ermland*, *T13*, *T10* and *T14* on 11 August 1942. Four days later, the two tankers attempted a breakout together, being escorted by two of the torpedo boats, each of whom carried an AA armament of one 3.7-cm (1.5-inch) and seven 2-cm (.8-inch) guns plus a single 10.5-cm (4.1-inch) weapon and three torpedo tubes. On 17 August the air patrols found them again. They were bombed during the night suffering enough damage to warrant their return to Bordeaux and La Pallice. Some of the long-range aircraft involved had been four-engined Halifaxes and Stirlings, specially loaned to Coastal from Bomber Command. The latter's opposition to their diversion from the main offensive against Germany had been particularly strong when several of the brand-new Lancasters were also transferred. Six of these carried out the last attack on 19 August. The loss of three of them for no apparent result seemed to bear out Bomber Command's belief that they were misused in maritime employment. From the German point of view, however, these reversals were rather more than mere hiccoughs. Any further interruption of supply tanker sailings could have a serious effect on U-boat operations in distant waters.

Apart from this the blockade runners' timetable was soon in full swing again:

8 August 1942: *Tannenfels* departed Yokohama.

20 August: *Dresden* departed Yokohama.

26 August: *Kulmerland* (HAPAG freighter; 7363 tons; Kapitän Pschunder) departed Dairen.

9 September: *Uckermark* departed Bordeaux.

14 September: *Regensburg* departed Kobe.

27 September: *Rhakotis* (HAPAG freighter; 6753 tons; Kapitän Jakobs) departed Yokohama.

28 September: *Rio Grande* departed Bordeaux.

1 October: *Pietro Orseolo* (Capitano Tarchioni) departed Bordeaux.

October: *Belgrano* (Hamburg-Südamerika freighter; 6095 tons), *Spichern* (ex-prize *Krossfonn*; supply tanker; 9323 tons), *Irene* (ex-prize *Silvaplana;* freighter; Kapitän Wendt), *Brake* (Jurgens van den Bergh tanker; 9925 tons; Kapitän Koelsbach), *Weserland* (ex-*Ermland*; HAPAG freighter; 6528 tons; Kapitän Krage) and *Karin* (ex-prize *Kota Nopan*; freighter; 7322 tons; Kapitän Klippe) departed Bordeaux.

21 October: *Charlotte Schliemann* arrived Yokohama.

23 October: *Ramses* (HAPAG freighter; 7983 tons; Kapitän Falcke) departed Kobe.

November: *Burgenland* (Kapitän Schutz) departed Bordeaux.

2 November: *Tannenfels* arrived Bordeaux.

3 November: *Dresden* arrived Bordeaux.

November: *Anneliese Essberger* departed Bordeaux.

7 November: *Kulmerland* arrived Bordeaux.

11 November: *Hohenfriedberg* (ex-prize tanker *Herborg;* 7892 tons; Kapitän Heidberg) departed Yokohama.

12 November: *Rossbach* (ex-prize tanker *Madrono;* 5894 tons); departed Kobe.

24 November: *Uckermark* arrived Yokohama.

29 November: *Cortellazzo* (Capitano Paladini) departed Bordeaux.

1 December: *Weserland* arrived Yokohama.

2 December: *Pietro Orseolo* arrived Kobe.

By now the blockade runners were being routed through the East Indies, across the Indian Ocean and round the Cape of Good Hope. A North Atlantic variation took them west of the Azores towards Newfoundland before turning east to run down the latitude of Bordeaux. While still in the Far East, and before embarking their final cargoes, they acted as general carriers, shipping various consignments between Dairen, Japan, Saigon and Singapore, aiding the Japanese war effort and earning yen for Germany's balance of payments. For example, *Ramses*, after serving as a prison ship for German raiders visiting Japan, was refitted and then loaded 3000 tons of whale oil for Bordeaux, plus building materials, ironwork and machinery. These items were discharged at Balikpapan, where she bunkered from oil lighters. The main cargo of 4000 tons of rubber, 40 tons of quinine, and tea, was embarked at Djakarta.

It was now becoming evident that all was not well with the programme. Things seemed to start going wrong round about the date of a battle which *Tannenfels* witnessed on 27 September 1942. She and the raider *Stier* had met at a remote South Atlantic rendezvous, when an American Liberty ship forged out of the mist. *Stier* was armed with six 15-cm (5.9-inch), two 3.7-cm (1.5-inch) and four 2-cm (.8-inch) guns, plus two torpedo tubes and two aircraft, but *Stephen Hopkins'* single 4-inch (10.2-cm) gun inflicted such damage on her assailant that the raider was sunk as well as her victim. *Tannenfels* had joined in with her automatic weapons whenever they bore, but her main contribution was to rescue the *Stier* survivors. The crew gave up their bunks to the thirty severely injured and *Tannenfels* set course for home. She had not been able to fuel before *Stier* had been sunk so she had to keep her speed down to 9 knots. By the latitude of the Azores, however, it was now or never, and speed was increased to 16 knots. Then a Royal Navy aircraft, evidently from a carrier just over the horizon, came in sight, followed by four destroyers. Would the scuttling charges have to be blown? Would the wounded have to take their chances in the lifeboats? No, *Tannenfels* appeared to be a British ship on an appropriate course for England. Again she was alone.

Then came a Sunderland, circling and circling at 300 feet, its crew obviously scrutinizing every detail of the ship. Anxiously, one, then several Germans, raised an arm, waved. They could see the pilot, his arm raised, waving. Satisfied, both parties went their separate ways. A number of torpedo boats met *Tannenfels* for her last lap through the Bay of Biscay and she duly delivered her cargo of rubber, edible oils, fats, wolfram, titanium, copper, wood oil, opium and quinine.

Tannenfels had been fortunate in her encounter with the Sunderland. The RAF was now stepping up its radar-equipped Biscay patrols, covering the flying boats and bombers with long-range fighters. All outward-bound and incoming vessels were escorted by the 3rd and 5th Torpedo Boat Flotillas, but even so *Belgrano* and *Spichern* were so badly damaged (the latter with depth-charges) that they had to abandon their voyages and put into El Ferrol, a neutral refuge which would soon be denied to them through British pressure on Spain. *Pietro Orseolo* escaped the strike directed at her, but *Anneliese Essberger* (whose codename was *Herstein*) had her propeller shaft jarred by a nearmiss. She kept going at a slightly reduced speed, carrying dyestuffs, cement, fireclay, forms for castings, bicycle parts, machinery and a small schnellboot. No. 3 Hold was empty, having been fitted with tanks for bringing back 1200 tons of vegetable oil.

Elsa Essberger due to sail, was hit in a combined Bomber and Coastal Command raid on shipping gathered in the Gironde estuary. Mines were also laid, and *Elsa Essberger* never went to sea again as a blockade runner.

On the other side of the world, *Regensburg* was proceeding through the constricted Sunda Strait when she was sighted by the US submarine *Searaven*. The resulting torpedo damage was not too serious. She was beached on Sumatra, then unloaded her cargo at Djakarta prior to being docked and repaired at Singapore.

Meanwhile, the word had gone out to Allied commanders in the South Atlantic that several southbound blockade runners would soon be passing through the narrows between Brazil and West Africa. Vice-Admiral Ingram (US Navy) and Rear-Admiral Pegram (Royal Navy) made their dispositions. At 0532 on 21 November 1942, the US cruiser *Cincinnati* was almost on the Equator when she got a radar contact at a range of nearly twelve miles. The stranger was then sighted by a lookout in Rear-Admiral O.M. Read's flagship *Milwaukee*. The two cruisers and the destroyer *Somers* steered to investigate.

It was daylight when they approached a grey-painted freighter whose ensign and reply proclaimed her Norwegian nationality, but *Skjelbred* was not on the C-in-C's list. She eventually stopped in response to signals at 0646. Her crew started to abandon ship and flames could be seen inside the pilot-house when a bridge door was opened. Covered by the cruiser's 6-inch (15.2-cm) armament, Commander A.C. Wood ordered his destroyer's boat to be launched from a distance of 500 yards. As it moved away from *Somers'* side, there were three huge explosions on board the stranger and debris flew high into the air. The boats were now being lowered, although one man rushed aft to haul down the Norwegian flag, while another defiantly hoisted the German ensign to the mainmast truck.

She was going down fast, but *Somers'* party scrambled aboard, forcing one of the Germans to accompany them. They found enough documents to prove she was *Anneliese Essberger*. There was also a dog which had been shot before the Germans abandoned him and the ship. The Americans returned to their boat and cast off, *Anneliese Essberger* having only a foot of freeboard aft. She then sank by the stern. The entire crew of sixty-two were rescued in the afternoon after air searches had shown that there were no U-boats or other runners in the area.

Neither *Milwaukee*, nor *Cincinnati* nor any of the warship or aircraft patrols saw any sign of the other rumoured blockade runners. The American cruisers' logs again reported breaking the monotony with convoy escorts, Crossing the Line ceremonies, rescuing exhausted albatrosses, and attending functions and parties ashore. The chief problem of reciprocal entertainment was making coffee in the syrupy way the Brazilians liked it.

The American cruisers were old, four-funnelled vessels not unlike the Australian cruiser *Adelaide*. At 2.16 pm on 28 November 1942, this warship was in company with the minesweeping sloops *Cessnock* and *Toowoomba*. Also present was the Dutch light cruiser *Jacob van Heemskerck*, which had been towed to Devonport for completion after the occupation of Holland. Together, they were escorting four merchantmen carrying oil refinery equipment from Free-mantle via the Chagos Archipelago to Abadan. They were about six hundred miles west of Australia near the Tropic of Capricorn, when Adelaide's masthead lookout sighted a merchant ship where no merchant ship should be. The two cruisers sheered out and six minutes later the vessel was turning away, broadcasting a raider alarm in the name of *Taujang*. At 3.43 pm, the stranger lowered two boats and emitted a dense cloud of smoke from an explosion right aft. Captain Esdaile immediately opened fire, partly because he suspected the ship was a disguised raider with a panic party, and partly because he wanted to hurry up the sinking and get back to the convoy. *Jacob van Heemskerck* also opened fire and the merchantman sank eight minutes later. Seventy-eight Germans, ten Norwegians, a pig and a dog were picked up. From these people it was learned that the ship's name was *Ramses*. Her lookouts had failed to see *Adelaide* first, because the cruiser's mast was camouflaged a pale duck-egg green.

Two days later it was the Italian *Cortellazzo* coming out of Biscay who was in trouble. By now, the torpedo boat escort had been scaled up. *Kondor* and *Falke* were larger and better-gunned but of prewar construction. *T22* and *T23* were two of the new Elbing-class, being built at the Schichau Yard in East Prussia. They were as big as other navies' destroyers, with a surface and AA armament to match. At high speed, they could reach 600 miles into the Atlantic. They saw no sign of the British submarines that patrolled the outer Bay, but off Cape Finisterre just before dark, they helped defend *Cortellazzo* against attack by a No. 10 RAAF Squadron Sunderland, which had sighted them earlier. But sooner, or later, the escort had to turn back. Next morning, 30 November 1942, *Cortellazzo* was alone.

Although she had already passed ahead of a large reinforcement convoy bound for North Africa, she still registered on the radar installed in the newly commissioned destroyer *Redoubt*, out on the starboard wing of the convoy with the Australian *Quickmatch*. The warships were ordered to investigate at high speed and soon sighted a large merchant ship, claiming to be the Swedish *Nanking* and transmitting on W/T. The Senior Officer in *Egret* reported this to the Admiralty at 1635. Their reply was timed 1726. 'SHIP IS NOT REPETITION NOT SWEDISH NANKING. ITALIAN CORTELLAZZO IS ESTIMATED TO BE IN ABOUT THIS POSITION' (ADM1/11710: *Identification of Suspicious Merchant Ships*).

Lieutenant-Commander Rhoades in *Quickmatch* ordered the Italian crew to abandon ship, but they replied that the weather was unsuitable. A shout of 'Get on with it!' (G.H. Gill, *Royal Australian Navy 1939–45*) over the loudhailer plus several 4.7-inch (119-mm) rounds from *Redoubt* caused a white flag to be run up, while Capitano Paladini gave the order to blow the charges and abandon ship. *Cortellazzo* was reluctant to sink, her end being hastened by a torpedo from *Redoubt*.

One German was lost and several picked up by *Quickmatch*, while *Redoubt* recovered the rest. Most were accommodated in the lower forward messdeck under armed guard, but the German officers who had been taking passage in *Cortallazzo* were berthed separately for their own safety. The Italians made no secret of their dislike of their erstwhile allies. Quite apart from the usual strains of any wartime partnership, most merchant seamen would feel aggrieved at being left in the lurch by short-ranged escorts that turned back just before they were needed. The Italians soon had their own chef preparing food, expressed their relief at being out of the war and did their best to be friendly with *Redoubt*'s ships's company. Nevertheless, they as well as the Germans were blindfolded when being landed at Gibraltar, just in case they later escaped with knowledge of the Rock's defences.

A fate similar to *Cortellazzo*'s befell the tanker *Germania* on 15 December 1942, after her torpedo boats had gone, but this time her nemesis was a destroyer from a northbound convoy. Because her tanks were empty, she stayed afloat after her scuttling charges had been blown. She was also torpedoed and shelled, and when last seen was on fire fore and aft.

For six hours on the morning of *Germania*'s departure from the Gironde on 12 December, the docks at Bordeaux had been rocked with explosions. As the echoes of the last died away about 1 pm, *Dresden* had sunk by the stern with holes torn in her after plates and her propeller shaft wrecked. *Tannenfels*' hold was flooded and she was heeling over at 24 degrees. *Portland* had been badly holed and *Alabama*, which was completing preparations as a blockade runner had been blasted by five underwater detonations. A tanker and a *sperrbrecher* (mine destructor vessel) had also been damaged. Some ships were on fire and their lists increased as French firemen pumped water into compartments unaffected by the blaze.

Later, the damaged ships were patched up by divers, raised, drydocked and repaired, but only *Portland* was able to continue her blockade running career. It was not only a serious blow to the programme, but also a considerable embarrassment to the German authorities. Had not Admiral Bachman (Naval C-in-C Western France) assured der Führer that nothing could touch the blockade runners in Bordeaux. And now—it must be some sort of mine, they reasoned.

And then, they found a canoe and six men. They were Royal Marines, in uniform, but on the orders of Admiral Bachman they were shot as spies and saboteurs.

Ten men in five canoes had been launched from the submarine *Tuna* about 12 miles off the Gironde on the night of 7/8 December 1942. In four nights they had paddled over 70 miles, concealed in dangerous discomfort during the days. RAF photographs had been used for the prior recommendation of suitable hiding-places. Two men were drowned early on and only two canoes made the final stealthy approach on the night of 11/12 December. Half-observed by one sentry who probably imagined he was seeing things, they used 6-foot poles to place limpet mines well below the surface on the ships' plates. Two Royal Marines survived and were passed through the French underground movement back to England. The Royal Marine Boom Patrol Detachment had struck where the Royal Navy and the RAF could not reach. In Bordeaux itself, as well as in the Bay of Biscay, Lord Selborne's promptings were having their effect.

14 Crisis Winter

The explosions in Bordeaux had been preceded by disaster in Yokohama. The tanker *Uckermark* had docked safely after supplying diesel oil to the raider *Michel* in the South Atlantic. On 30 November 1942, her crew were cleaning out her tanks before embarking her next liquid cargo. Each tank had to be steamed out for twenty-four hours and was then hosed down with hot water at high pressure. The work was arduous, each man being relieved after only five minutes in the tank. It was also hazardous, air and toxic fumes forming a highly explosive gas. Alongside *Uckermark* was *Thor*, taking in stores for her next foray against Allied shipping.

Then *Uckermark* blew up. *Thor* caught fire and was a total wreck. So was the German merchantman *Leuthen* and various harbour craft. What had caused it? Japanese saboteurs working for the Russians, some said. Most agreed with the enquiry's conclusion that the accident (which killed fifty-three of *Uckermark*'s crew) had arisen from the normal hazards of tank cleaning.

Neither *Uckermark* nor *Leuthen* would now be available as blockade runners, but this was not as serious a blow to the programme as the canoeists' raid on ships and cargoes at Bordeaux had been. So, departures and arrivals at the Oriental termini continued almost without pause, although sailings from the Gironde could not be resumed until the spring of 1943.

17 December 1942: *Doggerbank* departed Kobe.

20 December: *Irene* arrived Kobe.

23 December: *Brake* arrived Kobe.

30 December: *Karin* arrived Singapore.

31 December: *Rio Grande* arrived Kobe.

5 January 1943: *Weserland* departed Kobe.

12 January: *Burgenland* arrived Kobe.

20 January: *Irene* departed Kobe.

25 January: *Pietro Orseolo* departed Kobe.

28 January: *Rio Grande* departed Yokohama.

4 February: *Karin* departed Singapore.

6 February: *Regensburg* departed Djakarta.

7 February: *Burgenland* departed Kobe.

On Christmas Day 1942, *U410* met *Rhakotis* southwest of the Azores. The freighter had been on passage for three months and was carrying 4000 tons of rubber, 200 tons of textiles, zinc ore, lard, quinine bark, coconut oil and pearls valued at 50,000 yen for the Japanese Embassy in Berlin. Altogether it was the most expensive wartime cargo carried in a German ship, being worth 6,000,000 marks. For a week the two vessels remained in company, and then a representative from Australia's No. 10 Sunderland Squadron joined them, followed by a Hampden of No. 502 Squadron at St Eval. *HMS Scylla* was on her way, detached from a Gibraltar convoy. Intelligence—in particular the interception of signals to U-boats—had put the Allied forces in the right place at the right time.

On sighting the aircraft, *U410* dived, lost touch with her charge and played no further part in the proceedings. The two aeroplanes stayed out of range of *Rhakotis'* two 2-cm (.8-inch) oerlikons. While one kept in touch, the other found *Scylla* and, dropping a series of smoke bombs, signposted a pathway to the target.

The cruiser was sometimes called 'The Toothless Wonder.' Designed for five twin 5.25-inch (13.3-cm) turrets, these had been transferred to the Army for the defence of London and *Scylla* had therefore been completed with eight 4.5-inch (11.4-cm) guns. They were more than enough for *Rhakotis*. Kapitän Jakobs maintained a well-run ship (there were always fourteen lookouts on duty with 75-mm binoculars) but there was nothing he could do that afternoon west of Finisterre, with a cruiser standing off and shelling him until *Rhakotis* was a blazing wreck. *Scylla* recovered a few of the survivors, including Italians from other merchantmen in the Far East. *Rhakotis* eventually foundered about midnight, leaving eighty men to be recovered by two Spanish fishing boats. There was also one Briton, the only survivor out of three who had spent thirty-five days in a lifeboat in the South Atlantic before being spotted by *Rhakotis*.

Grossadmiral Raeder attributed this interception to the growing efficiency of British air patrols over the Bay of Biscay approaches. Certainly these were growing in strength and coverage, but it was not realized by the Germans that it was their own signals to U-boats which were telling the aircraft where to look. They thought that if there were any breaches of security, it must be the Italians' fault, adding another strain on a weakening alliance.

OKM now had several weeks in which to review and reorganize the arrangements for the passage of blockade runners through the Bay of Biscay and its approaches. No ship would be ready for departure before the end of February and none were now expected to arrive before then. The tanker *Rossbach* would not be coming. The failure of *Ermland* and *Spichern* to reach their allotted areas and the loss of *Uckermark*, was compromising the proposed U-boat operations in the Indian Ocean and South Atlantic. Accordingly, SKL ordered *Rossbach* to turn back to Djakarta and remain in the Far East as a supply tanker. The small NDL freighters *Bogota* and *Quito* would also be employed in this work.

On 30 January 1943, Grossadmiral Dönitz became head of the Kriegsmarine. Among the plans he outlined at his first conference with der Führer on 8 February 1943 was the strengthening of the Biscay forces. On this occasion, and on subsequent meetings, OKM stressed the necessity of building up maritime squadrons operating under Fliegerführer Atlantik. Not having any aircraft of their own, the Kriegsmarine could only make representations to the Luftwaffe for the co-operative employment of suitable aircraft. The number of long-range fighters, particularly Ju88s, was increased, but there were never enough armed reconnaissance and strike aircraft. As, at the same time, the Allies were reinforcing their squadrons, any Luftwaffe domination over the Bay, though formidable in appearance and effect, was only of temporary duration.

There was no administrative problem about the movement of the Kriegsmarine's own warships and that would be put in train at once. But before any of these measures could be implemented, the homeward-bound runners suffered two blows in quick succession.

BdU's dispositions for the protection of *Hohenfriedberg*'s return were the most extensive to date. From the latitude of the Azores onwards, which Kapitän Heidberg reached on 21 February 1943, a defensive circle was formed around the tanker, consisting of *U258*, *U264* and *U437*, keeping her in sight all the time. Meanwhile, *U172*, *U515* and *U508*, en route to their patrol areas, kept watch to the north of *Hohenfriedberg*'s track. For four days all went according to plan. Then, on 26 February, 500 miles southwest of Cape Finisterre, like a bird of ill-omen, appeared a four-engined Consolidated B-24 Liberator. The USAAF was in process of establishing an anti-submarine group at Port Lyautey.

Immediately the U-boats dived, driven underwater and rendered almost as impotent as if they had been sunk. Only *U264*, manoeuvring submerged at $7\frac{1}{2}$ knots, got a favourable glimpse of HMS *Sussex* swinging into position that evening. *U264* fired a spread of torpedoes, all of which missed as the cruiser changed course 90 degrees at a time, so that she zigzagged in a square box. Her 8-inch (20.3-cm) shells struck home and *Hohenfriedberg* spewed flame. When warship and aircraft and tanker had all disappeared from sight, *U264* surfaced and plucked the survivors from the February waves.

To the Germans it gave further proof of the ubiquity of Allied air power—or else incredibly bad luck that aircraft and warship patrol happened to coincide with *Hohenfriedberg*'s passage. Even worse luck was in store for *Doggerbank* and her 7000 tons of rubber, plus vegetable and fish oils from Japan, Saigon, Singapore and Djakarta. Increased strength of Allied air patrols persuaded the German authorities to open a new blockade route past the Azores. Appropriate U-boat dispositions were set in motion to be effective as from 15 March 1943. But Kapitän Schneidewind was pushing *Doggerbank* along at her best speed. She was running early and on 3 March was 1000 miles west of the Canaries. A U-boat was sighted on the surface and what seemed to be a correct exchange of signals took place. Which submarine that was, is not clear. What is certain, is that about two and a half hours later, *U43* operating against the North African supply route fired three torpedoes and sank what her capitan identified as a British liner, either *Dunnottar Castle* or *Dunedin Star*.

Twenty-six days later, the Spanish tanker *Campoamor* recovered an unconscious man from a Japanese-made dinghy and landed him in Venezuela. Living on flying fish, Fritz Kürt was the sole survivor of fifteen men who had got away from *Doggerbank*, sinking in three minutes after being struck by *U43*'s torpedoes. He related a harrowing tale of hunger, thirst and Kapitän Schneidewind's suicide after putting four men out of their misery with his pistol.

In March 1943, the promised reinforcements arrived in the Gironde to join the blockade runners' escort force. Commanded by Kapitän zur See H. Erdmenger, the 8th Destroyer Flotilla at first comprised *Z23*, *Z24*, *Z32* and *Z37*. They were generally known as the Narvik-Flotille in honour of the destroyers which had fought at Narvik in 1940. Kapitän zur See Erdmenger was himself a veteran of that battle. They were big (2600–3600 tons) and carried five 15-cm (5.9-inch) guns. It was hoped that the newly installed twin turret on the forecastle would provide a considerable forward punch. Their AA armament consisted of four 3.7-cm (1.5-inch) and fourteen 2-cm (.8-inch) automatic weapons. There were also eight torpedo tubes. They had a cruising range of 5000 miles and a maximum speed of 38 knots. They would be able to fight off clumsy four-engined bombers and handle any surface warship that dared enter the Bay of Biscay to interfere with the blockade runners under their protection. There were now over a dozen destroyers and torpedo boats available at any one time for surface protection with U-boats still being allocated for more distant duties. When BdU, Grossadmiral Dönitz had often criticized this activity as a misuse of his boats, but he continued the practice when he became OKM.

By now, *Regensburg*, *Pietro Orseolo*, *Karin* and *Irene* were coming north. *Weserland* was still far down in the South Atlantic, while *Rio Grande*, and *Burgenland* were only passing through the Indian Ocean. Accordingly, Kapitän Krage was ordered to mark time in the South Atlantic, while the reception of the nearer blockade runners was organized under the codename Arno. This programme would be co-ordinated with Operation Sacco, the despatch of four eastbound runners, the first since the Cockleshell Heroes' raid on Bordeaux.

In effect, the only incoming vessel to be directly involved would be *Pietro Orseolo*.

The other three (*Regensburg*, *Karin* and *Irene*) were routed much farther north, through the Denmark Strait (where *U191*, *U635* and *U469* were stationed) around Iceland and into Norwegian waters, under escort of the 6th Destroyer Flotilla.

Even before Operation Arno had begun, the US Navy was scratching one of the participants from the list. On 10 March 1943, a pilot from the escort carrier *Santee* spotted a Dutch merchant ship about 650 miles east of Natal in Brazil. While the destroyer *Livermore* stayed with the carrier, Rear-Admiral Read took the cruiser *Savannah* and the destroyer *Eberle* to investigate. They covered the 17 miles in just over half an hour. While *Savannah* stood off and covered the stranger with her fifteen 6-inch (15.2-cm) guns, *Eberle* went in close, reporting the merchantmen's appearance. There was something about the colour of her painted masts which prompted Rear-Admiral Read to make one of those dramatic signals which so often punctuate American naval history. 'YEAST FROM CACTUS NEVER MIND DUTCH FLAG PILE IN THERE THIS IS A RUNNER,' (NRS 1971/61: *US Atlantic Fleet Cruiser Division 2*).

The two-funnelled destroyer loosed a couple of 5-inch (12.7-cm) rounds as a warning and cleared away a boarding party. Immediately smoke appeared from the vessel. In spite of machine-gun fire from *Savannah*'s catapult aircraft, the crew started to abandon ship, their survival provisions including bread still oven-hot. Ignoring the spreading blaze, *Eberle*'s sailors scrambled aboard, having practised long for this eventuality. They searched for documents and scuttling devices. Others were clambering up a Jacob's ladder when a shattering explosion blasted the ship's side, disintegrating the American boat alongside and killing all but two of the boat's crew, one of the victims being swept into the hole in the sinking vessel. The men still on board got clear and the dazed survivors were picked up by another boat from *Eberle*. Altogether eight men were lost and two wounded.

The blockade runner sank, taking 2000 tons of tin ingots and 6000 tons of rubber with her. That was why *U174* could not find *Karin* when the submarine reached the appointed rendezvous to hand over a spare radar warning set and aerial.

This Metox equipment was already installed in U-boats picking up Allied radar transmissions and enabling them to dive before the approaching aircraft was in an attacking position. It could be something of a liability, registering impulses too weak to be reflected, so that U-boats could submerge before it was necessary with a resulting reduction in operational efficiency. On the other hand, it gave no warning of the new 10-cm wavelengths. Obviously the blockade runners could not dive but the warning would give the crew time to man the AA guns before a nocturnal or mist-shrouded attack. It was vital that the U-boats deliver this equipment, and signals were made to them stressing its importance, explaining the installation and designating rendezvous—all of which could be intercepted and deciphered. Both *Regensburg* and *Pietro Orseolo* received their Metox from *U161* west of the Azores on 23 and 26 March respectively.

Meanwhile *Osorno* had sailed from the Gironde, followed later in the month by the repaired *Portland* (under Kapitän Tünemann) and *Alsterufer*. On 28 March, Capitano Martinoli took *Himalaya* out of Bordeaux, escorted by *Falke*, *T2*, *T12*, *T18* and *T23*. Next day, when alone, she had to turn back west of Cape Finisterre because she was sighted by an enemy warship. By 30 March she had again been taken under torpedo boats' escort (this time *Kondor*, *T5*, *T9* and *T19*), and was returning to harbour. They thus passed the big destroyers *Z23* *Z24*, *Z32* and *Z37*, on their way to meet *Pietro Orseolo*.

They did not know that another Allied force had arrived in the Bay of Biscay. US Submarine Squadron (Subron) 50 was now based at Rosneath on the Clyde to assist in the interception of the iron ore, wolfram and contraband traffic from the Iberian peninsula to French ports. They had strict instructions not to interfere with neutral vessels, but Axis blockade runners were fair game. The Allies knew they were on their way, aerial reconnaissance having photographed the arrival of the 8th Zerstörer Flotille and the preparations for departure of eastward-bound vessels.

There was also intelligence from agents' reports and from the interception of U-boat signals. Overall control of operations against the blockade runners was vested in C-in-C Plymouth. The new cruiser *Newfoundland* and two destroyers were the first warships based there specifically for this work. Coastal Command was alerted, while Icelandic-based aircraft and Home Fleet ships took appropriate measures farther north. So it was that on 29/30 March the cruisers *Belfast* and *Glasgow* with their accompanying destroyers *Intrepid* and *Echo* were stationed on Patrol White in the middle of the Denmark Strait. Meanwhile *Bermuda* and *Athabaskan* were positioned between Iceland and the Fareoes. Each vessel was isolated in the cold darkness. The guns' crews were at night cruising stations, one 4-inch (10.2-cm) mounting being manned on each side of the ship. About half an hour after the Morning Watch had taken over, *Glasgow*'s radar picked up an unidentified blip on the screen. Action Stations was sounded, guns and searchlights being trained on the appropriate bearing. When close enough, 4-inch (10.2-cm) starshell was fired and the searchlight shutters opened, revealing a single-funnelled merchantman. She was challenged and ordered to stop or be sunk. Captain E.M. Evans-Lombe later told a newspaper reporter that he knew it could be none other than a German ship, although he did not elaborate on the reasons for his certainty. He explained how he intended to direct the stranger into more sheltered waters, where he could not have prevented scuttling, but would have been able to save the ship's company. As in most wartime reports for public consumption, the German's subsequent actions were then described as 'panicky' or 'damned stupid.'

The stranger flashed back 'I stop,' but within minutes there was a series of explosions and the crew began lowering boats and jumping over the side. Although the sea was fairly calm, a heavy swell quickly carried them away from the settling ship. She was not going down very fast, and *Glasgow* could not wait too long because U-boats were known to be about. Captain Evans-Lombe ordered the Gunnery Officer to exercise the 6-inch and 4-inch (15.2-cm and 10.2-cm) armament on the derelict, taking care to avoid hitting the lifeboats. The shells were rammed home to the accompaniment of the customary naval orders, which in the best tradition of mariners' tales for war correspondents, were translated into yells of 'Here's one for Coventy,' 'Here's another for Plymouth,' 'And another for Birmingham.'

There was not much time for any exclamations. The blockade runner suddenly upended and went down stern-first in the dawning gloom. By now thick snow showers were coursing over the rising sea. An officer in one of the lifeboats seemed to be threatening the others with a pistol, trying to make them keep clear of the cruiser. The boat then fouled *Glasgow*'s wallowing stern, throwing the occupants into the freezing water. Six men were recovered by means of scrambling nets (confirming that it was *Regensburg* that had been sunk) before *Glasgow* made off, leaving 112 to an icy fate. Neither *Regensburg*'s covering U-boats, nor the 6th Zerstörer-Flotille saw anything of the action.

However, the 8th Zerstörer-Flotille was being more enterprising farther south. On 31 March 1943, *Z23*, *Z24*, *Z32* and *Z37* reached 41° North/15° West, the most southerly position ever reached by any German destroyer during World War II. They were so far out that Capitano Tarchioni of *Pietro Orseolo* assumed they must be British. The four Narviks beat off frequent attacks by Beauforts and Torbeaus, shooting down five of them, but on 1 April 1943, an American enemy was lying in wait.

At 2.20 am Lieutenant-Commander Edgar J. MacGregor III, took *Shad* in on the surface, making his approach by radar. The water was highly phosphorescent, but the submarine's bow wave was not seen and at 3.42 am all six bow tubes were fired at the five blips showing on the radar screen. Even as five explosions split the night, *Shad* was swinging to fire two of the after tubes. This resulted in another detonation, followed by three more which did not sound like depth-charges or torpedoes self-destructing at the end of their run. It was believed that the blockade runner and two of the escorts had been sunk and Lieutenant-Commander MacGregor was awarded the British Distinguished Service Cross. However, at this stage of the war, US magnetic pistols were notoriously unreliable. Only one torpedo had hit, blowing a hole in *Pietro Orseolo*'s starboard side. She kept going at half speed with bales of rubber floating out. Every single one was a loss to the war effort. So, whenever possible, the destroyers stopped engines briefly to recover a couple more bales from the sea. As *Pietro Orseolo* came up the Gironde on 2 April, she left a buoyant trail behind her. Nearly all the 1500 tons in No. 2 Hold were lost. Even in harbour, right until she entered drydock, an occasional bale of rubber bobbed free and floated away to be washed up on some riverine strand. French civilians did very well out of the rewards offered for this salvaged material. The Germans also promised 90 pesetas per kilo for rubber recovered along the Spanish coast, but the Spanish government kept whatever was found there.

Pietro Orseolo's compatriot *Himalaya* set out once more—from La Pallice— on 9 April, protected by no less than eight warships, *Z23*, *Z24*, *Z32*, *Kondor*, *T2*, *T5*, *T22* and *T23*. This was the strongest escort to date, but it was still not powerful enough. After numerous air attacks, *Himalaya* had to return. *Osorno*, too, had been sighted, but she kept going, and broke out into the South Atlantic. The 2729-ton *Alsterufer*, owned by Robert M. Sloman and commanded by Kapitän Piatek, was able to make her passage unobserved. *Portland* also seemed to be having a fortunate voyage.

Meanwhile *Irene*, coming north, had received radar warning apparatus from *U174* when northwest of the Azores. Keeping clear of Allied convoy routes, she made for France, but on 10 April she was still 275 miles out from Cape Finisterre. So far she had seen only an Allied liner in the distance, but she then exchanged recognition signals with a Focke-Wulf Fw200c. For some reason, the pilot did not mention that for two and a half hours he had circled a British warship only a short distance away.

Earlier in 1943, the minelaying cruiser *Adventure* had delivered a cargo of mines to Gibraltar for laying in the Mediterranean by faster vessels. *Adventure* herself was not speedy enough for such tasks. She could do only 27 knots, but that was enough to allow *Irene* no escape when the two ships sighted each other with 17 miles between them. 'Be careful,' signalled *Irene*. 'I saw a submarine this morning' but at 9000 yards, Captain Bowes-Lyon flashed 'WBA', the standard combined International Code signal meaning 'STOP DO NOT LOWER BOATS DO NOT RADIO DO NOT SCUTTLE IF YOU DISOBEY I SHALL OPEN FIRE! (ADM1/12476: *HMS Adventure Interception and Sinking of MV Silvaplana*).

Within five minutes and without waiting for the ship to stop, 158 men had abandoned her in one motor-boat, six lifeboats and two floats. Many had rope burns on their hands. *Irene*'s bridge was seen to be on fire, the flames being spread by an explosion in the superstructure. This was followed by the main scuttling charges, so that *Irene* sank at 1731, taking raw rubber, zinc and tinned tunny fish with her. The men now afloat may have included British prisoners. Even if they were all Germans, they would be able to reach Spain quite easily in this calm weather and could then get home to help the war effort. So, Captain Bowes-Lyon dropped three depth-charges to frighten off any U-boats in the area and quickly gathered up the survivors. The majority of them were submariners returning from the Far East; their capture eliminated the equivalent of two full crews from the Battle of the Atlantic.

By now the former Vichy French forces were working with the Allies again. The light cruiser *Georges Leygues* (named after the inter-war Minister of Marine who had revitalized the French Navy) was one of those based at Dakar under Vice-Admiral Collinet. A British Naval Liaison Officer plus five telegraphists and visual signalmen were appointed to each ship to handle Royal Navy codes, the French ones having been compromised during the Occupation. The British were more readily accepted if their fluency and French accent were good—as applies to all Anglo-French relationships. In at least one instance, it helped to break potential tensions when a BNLO was of Scottish, rather than English, ancestry.

Shortage of oil and political considerations had restricted the time French warships could spend at sea under the Vichy government. Officers and ratings had together concentrated on making sure that standards of drill, cleanliness and discipline were maintained. They ended their period of armed neutrality with their early-war view of themselves as 'Guardians of the Honour of France' considerably strengthened. As one British report stated—strangely echoing a German opinion about the French—'They want to fight and don't much care who they fight against' (FO371/36002/Z9586: *Attitude of Men of the French Navy, 14 August 1943*). For two years, French merchant seamen had had to submit to British contraband control; now the French Navy could start harassing Axis merchantmen and warships.

Capitaine de Vaisseau Robert Jaujard was what is known in motoring circles as 'a positive driver.' Under his command, *Georges Leygues* (9120 tons full load) creamed in and out of Dakar, 84,000 shp, stopping the ship in exactly the right position. At 1 am on 13 April, as the moon was setting in a cloudy sky, one of his lookouts—there was no radar—sighted a ship about five miles distant. Capitaine de Vaisseau Jaujard steered *Georges Leygues* so that the vessel was silhouetted against the declining moon. There was no answer to the challenge and they were expecting *Portland*, but the Frenchmen had never seen an American Liberty ship and it would not do to make a mistake. Her next move seemed to indicate her hostility. The stranger made smoke behind which screen she turned 180 degrees. Capitaine de Vaisseau Jaujard had anticipated this movement, paralleled her course, and was waiting when she emerged into the clear. He decided that if she were an Allied ship, she ought not to behave so suspiciously and had been given fair warning. He was prepared to accept credit or blame for his action and ordered the starboard 90-mm (3.5-inch) mounting to open fire. Its crew were so expert that they hit the target amidships with their second salvo. The stranger exploded, thus ending any chance of capture. It could still be a friendly merchantman loaded with munitions, not a blockade runner fitted with scuttling charges, but the cruiser could not linger because of the danger from U-boats. It was not until dawn that fifty-one survivors were gathered up from two lifeboats, Capitaine de Vaisseau Jaujard going full ahead as soon as the last man put his foot on the ladder hung over the side. The Executive Officer's shout from the quarterdeck of '*Portland!*' could be heard on the bridge. Capitaine de Vaisseau Jaujard dismissed his success as 'an attack by a tank against a boy armed with a cap pistol' (*Chicago Daily News*, May 1943). He looked forward to swapping punches with a strong adversary in the Mediterranean.

French and American cruisers in the narrows between Brazil and Africa, British cruisers in the Atlantic and Denmark Strait, British and American aircraft and submarines in the Bay of Biscay—these were the agencies that had sunk, damaged or turned back all but three of the past ten blockade runners in both directions. Only in Biscay could the Kriegsmarine provide substantial escort—and even that ought to be strengthened before any more runners made the final approach towards European waters. Besides, it was now well into April; the North Atlantic nights were getting shorter and calmer. Accordingly, SKL ordered *Weserland*, *Rio Grande* and *Burgenland* to turn back to Yokohama, Kobe and Djakarta respectively, being joined in Japanese ports on 4 and 19 June 1943 by *Osorno* and *Alsterufer*.

15 Undersea Blockade Runners

It was a depressing situation that Axis blockade runners found themselves in in the middle of 1943. It seemed impossible that merchantmen could get through the Indian and Atlantic Oceans now bordered by hostile bases and then penetrate the Allied blockade of Nazi-Occupied Europe. Few could outrun warships and none were faster than aircraft. Radar had given both nocturnal and bad-weather vision. No escort seemed powerful enough to guarantee safe arrival if the runner were intercepted and protection could certainly not be provided much beyond inner Biscay. Even the blockade runners' trick of putting on a bold face and bluffing their way past inquisitive patrols was less likely to work now.

On 8 June 1943, the Allies introduced the Checkmate System, which involved estimating the daily position of every independent ocean-going merchant ship in the world. During the first half of the war, warships proceeding to sea were told which vessels they were likely to see, the situation being updated by signal from the shore during their patrol. No matter how well the plot was maintained, strange but bona fide merchantmen were encountered, proceeding independently on ocean trade routes, who had not been reported to local commands. Only 50 per cent of British ships answered the challenge with their secret signal letters correctly, let alone foreigners. Ships' names were sometimes spelled out improperly so that they could not be found in alphabetical lists—which did not always contain the latest construction or change of name. At the same time, Axis intelligence told their captains which ships would be the best to impersonate in particular areas.

Under the Checkmate System, an intercepting warship or aircraft now used the Merchant Ship Description Code and Merchant Ship Silhouette Characteristics Register plus its own merchant ship plot and secret signal, to identify the stranger. In most cases this was sufficient, but if inconclusive, a plain language signal was made to the Admiralty or to the local C-in-C. It read 'EMERGENCY CHECK (stranger's signal letters) (alleged name) (position—by lettered coordinates).' The reply, usually within a few minutes was of three types:-

'MATE TRUE'—ship could be there.

'MATE FALSE'—impossible for a genuine ship of that name to be in that position.

'MATE DOUBTFUL'—further investigation desirable.

Even though bona fide merchantmen often ignored visual signals and waited until within hailing distance before replying to challenges, warships should not get that close. A warning shot at long range invariably produced some response. If the vessel were then revealed as an enemy blockade runner, automatic fire directed at the bridge and the boats while still at the davits might prevent scuttling. However, the priority was to deprive the enemy of her cargo, by sinking if necessary. The need for capture to make up lost tonnage or production, was not important at this stage of the war. Cruisers should keep at full speed and never stop to pick up survivors. Destroyers and smaller warships could recover men for interrogation, but it would be better to leave them in the water. Other German vessels might then come to the rescue, thus affording further targets. Intercepting aircraft must keep in touch and summon help.

The only way the blockade runner could escape was by making his ship invisible; and so, as in World War I, the German naval command again considered the employment of undersea blockade runners.

During World War II, all navies utilized submarines for the emergency transport of stores and passengers through areas too hazardous for surface or aerial communication. In 1940, the Germans themselves had used U-boats for the delivery of aircraft fuel, ammunition, guns and gear to Norway. After the loss of so many supply ships in 1941, the Kriegsmarine had been forced to employ big minelaying boats as submarine tankers and spare torpedo carriers. A programme of special construction and conversion was then begun, instead of the ad hoc adaptation of operational boats. The Type VIIF was some thirty feet longer than the Type VIIC, enabling the stowage and transfer of twenty-five spare torpedoes, in addition to its normal complement. *U180* and *U195* were the only representatives of Type IXD1. Their experimental high-speed diesels proved so troublesome that they were taken off operations, refitted with new engines, and had their torpedo tubes and some batteries removed so that they emerged as submarine tankers with a capacity of 252 tons. The Type XIV boats (ten of them) were nicknamed 'broad-beamed.' Shorter than the Type IXD1, their tanks could hold 432 tons of fuel. Another four were cancelled. Enthusiastic designers got rather carried away with the Types XV and XVI, the latter reaching 5000 tons. They were intended to serve as submersible repair ships as well as supply vessels. Considering the ubiquity of Allied air patrols, it was fortunate for their crews that they never left the drawing board. Nor did the 2000-ton Type XIX tankers. The main combat U-boat for late war-service was intended to be the streamlined, snorkel-fitted Type XXI. Supply versions were designated XXID, XXIE, XXIT and XXIV.

Germany's Axis partners also used submarines as transports. For the Japanese, it became the method of supplying isolated garrisons, the big cruiser submarines carrying landing craft, rubber boats and amphibious tanks (stressed for depths of 200 feet) on deck to ferry stores ashore. When too hazardous to wait, the items were floated ashore on a rising tide in the hope that somebody would find them. The service proved so vital that special vessels were laid down for it. The twelve boats of the *I361*-class could carry 60 tons of cargo internally and another 22 tons externally. Their greatest attribute was a submerged range of 120 miles at 3 knots. Only *I373* of the improved class was completed, able to take 260 tons of cargo, including 150 tons of petrol. One of the world's biggest submarines at that date was *I402* with a full load displacement of 5223 tons. She was completed as a fuel supply boat, contrasting with the twelve craft of the *Ha101*-class, carrying 60 tons in a 370-ton hull. All these transport submarines were given priority in Japanese ship construction, but steel shortages and the even higher priority accorded to suicide craft resulted in the cancellation of another 325 boats. Dissatisfied with these cutbacks and always resentful of dependence on the Navy, the Japanese Army embarked on its own programme of submarine building. There were three classes, *Yu1*, *Yu1001* and *Yu2001*, ranging in size from 273 to 392 tons, although all carried 40 tons of cargo. About thirty or so were completed. Like the Navy boats, they were intended for military logistics, not as undersea merchantmen maintaining the flow of strategic raw materials to civilian industry. It was the Japanese Navy, however, which demonstrated the feasibility of underwater communication between the Far East and Europe.

I30 was a cruiser submarine with a displacement of 2198 tons. She had a streamlined aircraft hangar forward of the conning tower and could travel 16,000 miles at 16 knots without refuelling. She departed Penang in Malaya on 20 April 1942, in company with the armed raiders *Aikoku Maru* and *Hokoku Maru* from whom she refuelled at sea. After reconnoitring various Indian Ocean ports, Chu-sa (Commander) Endo rounded the Cape of Good Hope and headed northwards. Preceded by German minesweepers, *I30* entered the U-boat base at Lorient on 5 August 1942. Operation Kirschblüte (Cherry Blossom) it was called. With a return cargo, *I30* was back in Penang on 9 September 1942, calling at Singapore on 11 October 1942. Her cargo never reached Japan. Two days later *I30* was mined just outside Singapore.

Meanwhile the Italians had found submarines so useful for maintaining links between Italy, Libya and the Dodecanese, that they decided to build special boats for the traffic between western Europe and Japan, as well as for the trans-Mediterranean supply routes. On 20 July 1942, the first of twelve R-class submarines was laid down at the Tosi Yard in Taranto. They could carry 610 tons of cargo on a standard displacement of 1300 tons. Two sets of diesels and electric motors gave a speed of 13 knots, 6 knots submerged. The ship's company of sixty-three had three 20-mm (.8-inch) guns for defence. The first two were due to be launched on 21 and 28 March 1943, and would be named *Romolo* and *Remo* respectively. They would be commissioned three months later.

Obviously the Kriegsmarine was aware of these developments. They had also been reviewing U-boat deployment in the Far East since 1941. So far this had been inhibited by the short range of most boats (the Type VIIC could reach some 3000 miles only from its base), by the difficulties of arranging distant supply and by Admiral Dönitz's belief that it was a diversion from the North Atlantic Tonnage War.

The introduction of the Type IXD2, with a cruising range of 23,700 miles reopened the debate just as the Allied defences in the Atlantic seemed to be strengthening, and as the Japanese were suggesting Penang or Sabang (a Sumatran island) as Indian Ocean U-boat bases. They were also requesting the delivery of two German U-boats to serve as prototypes for similar Japanese construction. Grossadmiral Dönitz did not like this idea, but he was overruled by der Führer who wanted to keep the Japanese happy and supplying rubber. A U-boat was easier to replace than machine-tools.

No doubt all these matters were in Grossadmiral Dönitz's mind as he explained his blockade-running measures for 1943 to Hitler on 8 February 1943. The Type XX U-boat was being designed specifically for Far Eastern traffic. Two hundred were on order, displacing 2708 tons each. Their eight cargo holds could contain 800 tons of oil or dry goods, and they would have a range of 13,000 miles at 12 knots.

Until they arrived in service, transport could be undertaken by the use of converted Italian submarines, considered too unwieldy for operations against heavily defended Atlantic convoys. Their large conning towers gave them too obvious a silhouette and many were armed with two large guns whose infrequent employment hardly justified the resulting loss in underwater speed and silence. With Supermarina's agreement, work was begun as submarines returned to their base at Bordeaux. At first the Germans wanted to man the boats themselves, and then suggested that they be decommissioned as merchantmen, but Capitano Grossi at Betasom refused both requests. In exchange, the Italians' front-line force in the Battle of the Atlantic would be maintained by the transfer of a number of newly completed German U-boats.

Enrico Tazzoli, Giuseppe Finzi, Barbarigo, Comandante Cappellini, Archimede, Alpino Bagnolini, Reginaldo Giuliani, Leonardo da Vinci, Luigi Torelli and *Ammiraglio Cagni* were of seven different classes, completed between 1936 and 1941. The largest was *Ammiraglio Cagni* displacing 1504 tons. The idea was that they should rendezvous with freighters somewhere southeast of Madagascar to transfer cargoes and return. This area was the normal limit for normal

U-boats then operating off South Africa, whose tanks were topped up by 'milch cow' submarine tankers.

In addition several French submarines had been seized by the Germans at Bizerta in December 1942 and then handed over to the Italians. Four of these were scheduled for conversion as transports. They were all the same 974-ton class—*Phoque*, *Requin*, *Espadon* and *Dauphin*. They were renumbered *FR111*, *FR113*, *FR114* and *FR115*. Work on the first was completed very quickly, but on 28 February 1943 she was sunk by air attack off Sicily.

The first eastbound U-boat transport expedition had been planned some time previously, and was only awaiting an astrologically auspicious sailing date—9 February 1943. Korvettenkapitän Musenberg was not particularly superstitious, but his two passengers were. Subhas Chandra Bose, the Indian nationalist, had made his way to Berlin, whence he was to travel out to the Far East to raise an army from Indian prisoners of war, fight alongside the Japanese and liberate India from the British. Besides his Muslim ADC, *U180* would also be carrying plans and samples for new weapons and equipment, plus a large quantity of special chemicals which, when released in water, produced a mass of effervescing bubbles. Known to the Germans as 'Bolde' and to confused Allied asdic operators as a 'pill,' it produced a similar echo to a U-boat. Now this device would be available to Japanese submariners.

U180's diesels were more trouble than they were worth. When surfaced the boat was virtually invisible in a greyish-blue fog, itself a suspicious phenomenon to a training Anson which was fired on and kept its distance. Two vessels were attacked, Chandra Bose suffered seasickness and once fell overboard. Otherwise the voyage out and home was uneventful. The actual transhipment was carried out 180 miles southeast of Madagascar on 26–27 April 1943. In exchange *I29* sent over Oriental gold, quinine and examples of the latest Japanese equipment, conversations being conducted in an exasperating mixture of German, Japanese and English. *I29* took Chandra Bose to Penang, whence he flew on to Japan. *U180*, now carrying an uninvited selection of Far Eastern insect life, returned to Bordeaux on 3 July 1943.

Meanwhile plans were being prepared for the despatch of Gruppe *Monsun*. These operational U-boats were not to attract attention by attacking ships en route, unless the target were of exceptional significance. Beyond Africa, they would undertake normal patrols widening, their area of vision by towing Bachstelze helicopter-kites at a height of 400 feet. Their range would be extended by the supply tankers *Brake* and *Charlotte Schliemann*, the latter also being employed in the transport of edible oils from South-East Asia to Japan. Their torpedoes expended, the *Monsun* boats would refit at Penang and load a cargo of rubber, opium and other products. Even the food containers were made of pure zinc which could be recycled in Europe. With a couple of torpedoes for emergencies, they would return through the dangerous waters of the Atlantic.

From May 1943 onwards, it was a complicated programme of Italian transports, Japanese movements and *Monsun* U-boats which can be summarized as follows:-

10 May: *U511* (Type IXC) departed France, carrying Vice-Admiral Nomura (the Japanese Naval Attaché). She arrived at Kure on 7 August 1943. Next month *U511* was commissioned into the Imperial Japanese Navy as *Ro500*. After all the effort of getting her there and in spite of their talent for facsimile production, the Japanese decided that she was too complicated to copy.

11 May: *Comandante Cappellini* departed Bordeaux. Like the other Italian transports she was carrying stores, equipment and torpedoes for the *Monsun* base at Penang plus items for Japan. A typical cargo of 160 tons included mercury, steel and aluminium bars, welding steel, ammunition, bomb prototypes, 2-cm (.8-inch) guns, bombsight and tank blueprints. They could accommodate up to a dozen passengers, unhappy at the vessel's $3\frac{1}{2}$–6 per cent reserve buoyancy, instead of the customary 20–25 per cent. No Axis merchantmen were available for mid-ocean transhipment, so they would have to go on to Penang or Sabang, and then Singapore. Unarmed, except for machine-guns, they would be escorted through the Molucca Strait by the sloop *Eritrea*. *Comandante Cappellini* arrived Singapore on 13 July 1943. There the submarines' cargoes would be exchanged for zinc (44–70 tons), rubber (110–155 tons), wolfram (5 tons), quinine (2 tons), opium (2 tons), bamboo, rattan, and more passengers.

16 May: *Reginaldo Giuliani* departed Bordeaux, arriving at Singapore on 1 August 1943.

21 May: *Enrico Tazzoli* left Bordeaux, to be bombed and sunk in the Bay of Biscay.

11 June: *U200* (Type IXD2) sailed from Norway. The first of Gruppe *Monsun*, she was sunk by a PBY Catalina southwest of Iceland.

17–19 June: *Barbarigo* bombed and sunk in the Bay of Biscay after leaving Bordeaux.

18 June: *Luigi Torelli* departed Bordeaux. Southeast of the Cape of Good Hope she was met and fuelled by *U178* (a Type IXD2 boat) which had been ordered to remain in the Indian Ocean instead of going home. Together, the two submarines arrived at their Far Eastern base on 26 August 1943. Fregattenkapitän Wilhelm Dommes then became commander at Penang, with satellite facilities at Singapore, Djakarta, Surabaja and Kobe. It could hardly be said that this station was a happy one for any of the three Axis navies. Instead of uniting them, the physical discomforts of sickness and un-familiar food, the operational disadvantages of poor fuel and primitive facilities, the attitude of the civilian population divided between hatred and sycophancy, drove the three nationalities even farther apart. The Japanese

were not interested in the European war. They restricted German and Italian use of the Singapore Swimming Club and blamed all Westerners for American successes in the Pacific. The Germans were contemptuous of the Japansee and furious at their glad repetition of news stories about Soviet victories. The Italians took a poor view of Japanese aircraft recognition (four engines must be British or American) and were much impressed by Indonesian children who knelt before them asking forgiveness for supporting the Japanese against the Americans. The Germans were patronizing towards the Italians who were delighted when the Japanese arranged a screening of the film *The Great Dictator*, in which Charlie Chaplin mocked an autocratic ruler with a more than a passing resemblance to Adolf Hitler.

26/27 June: *I8*, a 2231-ton Japanese boat, left Penang. Besides her own complement of 100, she was accommodating forty-eight men to crew *U1224*, being built in Hamburg. During the voyage, Captain Uchino met *I10*, to top up his tanks, and *U161*. It took four hours to install the German radar warning equipment, and then *I8* was on her way again. At this time, the Luftwaffe's glider-bombs were achieving some success against British patrols in the Bay of Biscay, which had to be withdrawn farther out. This probably helped *I8*'s passage through the Bay, although one escort group depth-charged a series of contacts for sixteen hours, reporting a number of bales of rubber floating in a spreading slick of diesel. However, *T24*, *T22* and *T25* escorted *I8* into Lorient at the end of August 1943.

29 June–8 July: *U847* (Type IXD2) sailed from Norway. The rest of Gruppe *Monsun* (all Type IXC) and the Italian *Ammiraglio Cagni* departed from French ports. Damaged by ice in the Denmark Strait, *U847* headed for France. *U514*, *U506* and *U509* were all sunk in the Atlantic by aircraft, which also badly damaged *U462*, one of the special Type XIV supply boats. Two more submarine tanker losses meant that *U516* had to transfer her fuel to the survivors and return, leaving *U168*, *U183*, *U188*, *U532* and *U533* to enter the Indian Ocean as planned. *U533* was sunk while on patrol there.

5 September: *I8* moved round to Brest, where she loaded torpedo and aircraft engines, AA guns and equipment, and ten German advisers. Another strong escort (Operation Flieder—Lilac) took her out until she was able to dive and proceed alone, surviving an air attack in mid-Atlantic. From 10 to 14 November 1943, a powerful air and sea search hunted her off South Africa, picking up occasional D/F bearings on her signals, but the last one showed that Captain Uchino had escaped the net by remaining submerged during daylight hours. *I8* eventually reached Japan.

By now the situation had been altered by the Italian armistice of 8 September 1943. All merchantmen within Germany's sphere of influence were promptly commandeered. Their crews were given the option of sailing under the Nazi flag or of being marched off to prison. Most chose the latter. The submarine *Ammiraglio Cagni* forsook her *Monsun* operations (she had not yet been converted as a transport) and put into South Africa. *Comandante Cappellini* was seized by the Japanese at Sabang, *Reginaldo Giuliani* and *Luigi Torelli* at Singapore. All three were handed over to German crews and renumbered *UIT24*, *UIT23* and *UIT25*. *Alpino Bagnolini*'s conversion had just been completed, while *Giuseppe Finzi*'s was still in progress. Both were requisitioned by the Germans at Bordeaux as *UIT22* and *UIT21*. *Archimede* and *Leonardo da Vinci* had both been sunk earlier in 1943 before work had begun. A similar fate had befallen *Remo* and *Romolo* on their maiden voyages in July 1943. The other R-boats were never completed, nor was the conversion of the former French submarines which had passed into Italian ownership.

Altogether, the achievements of 1943 did not bode well for the future of undersea blockade runners from the Far East. Outward-bound items may have been of interest to Japanese technicians, but German industry had hardly benefitted from the minute quantities of raw materials that had been delivered by the three boats that had arrived in France. Perhaps more practical amounts would be forthcoming if enough submarine freighters could be built. But it would be some time before these would be completed, and even some time before Gruppe *Monsun* was ready to return at the end of its combat effectiveness. In the meantime, several large consignments of certain commodities—above all rubber—were needed now. And the only way was by surface ship—even the damaged *Pietro Orseolo* had unloaded 5100 tons of rubber, far more than had come by submarine runners.

The problem was, which ships could be used apart from the five that had arrived in Japan at the end of the last winter's blockade running. There were nine in Bordeaux, but they would have to be prepared and then get out to the Far East before bringing back a return cargo. At one time it was suggested that *Lutzow*, *Admiral Scheer* and the aircraft carrier *Graf Zeppelin* be used, but nothing came of this. Quite apart from the work involved in their conversion, it is hard to imagine such large, unmistakable warships passing unmolested from the Baltic, through the North Atlantic convoy routes, around the world and back again. Knowing Hitler's vehement opinions about risking capital ships unnecessarily, even the most enthusiastic officer would be unlikely to hazard the Kriegsmarine's whole future by broaching such an impracticable scheme. There had been several merchant ships hiding in neutral Goa, but in the early hours of 9 March 1943 eighteen members of the Calcutta Light Horse and the Calcutta Scottish had secretly steamed a barge into the port to destroy a clandestine transmitter on board the freighter *Ehrenfels*. During the confusion, the crews of other ships laid up there believed they were also under attack. They therefore ignited the kerosene and incendiary devices they had prepared, blew scuttling charges and opened the seacocks. The Hansa *Ehrenfels*, *Drachenfels* and *Braunfels* settled blazing on the bottom of the harbour, together with Lloyd-Triestino's *Anfora*. None of these would now be able to break out and make for Japanese waters.

Indeed, there were very few neutral ports where German merchantmen were still safe. Country after country declared war or broke off diplomatic relations with the Axis powers, which meant instant confiscation of any shipping which had been sheltering there since 1939–40. There were some in Portuguese harbours, but it was now obvious that they were watched so closely by agents or warships, that they could make no move without it being known to the Allies. In any case, many of them were not the most youthful of vessels. They had been laid up for years and would require major refit before attempting a serious voyage. Accordingly the companies began to sell off these ships to firms of local nationality, the currency or credit being used to obtain easily transportable items of value to the war economy.

By now Germany's merchant marine had lost so many ships through enemy action or through extravagant Kriegsmarine and Wehrmacht charter or requisition, that the Hansa Programme was instituted by Reichskommissar Kauffmann to construct standard merchant ships of 3000, 5000 and 9000 tons deadweight. They were allocated to shipping companies according to their share of the traffic and were principally employed in the Swedish iron ore trade, which continued until the Swedish government closed its harbours to Axis shipping in September 1944. The Hansa vessels would also be available for postwar victory services, and until then would participate in blockade running between Europe and the Far East. However, priority was assigned to so many other projects (U-boats were the most important in shipbuilding) that the Hansa Programme was not as fruitful as had been hoped. Under the new direction of John T. Essberger, fifty-eight ships were launched, but none served as blockade runners.

So, it would be up to the veterans of the Oriental run, *Alsterufer*, *Burgenland*, *Osorno*, *Rio Grande* and *Weserland*, and preparations were begun for their loading, routing and reception.

16 Desperate Gamble

Once again all the customary instructions were sent out to U-boats, mine-sweepers and Fliegerführer Atlantik. Kapitän zur See Erdmenger's destroyers and torpedo boats were reinforced by the arrival at Bordeaux of *Z27* and *ZH1*, formerly a Dutch destroyer under construction when Rotterdam was captured in 1940. Completed by the Germans, her main armament comprised five 12-cm (4.7-inch) guns and eight torpedo tubes.

Once again the other side learned what was happening from agents' reports, photographic reconnaissance and radio interception, other codes now being broken besides the signals to U-boats. The Allies had two further operational advantages. The neutral Portuguese were permitting British warships and aircraft to be based at the Azores, while the US Navy's airfield on Ascension was now fully in service; thus the North and South Atlantic gaps had been closed.

The board was ready, the first move in this worldwide chess game being made on 2 October 1943. *Osorno* slipped out of Kobe, followed two days later by *Alsterufer* (also from Kobe) and *Rio Grande* from Yokohama. *Weserland* and *Burgenland* both sailed from Yokohama on 26 and 29 October respectively.

The first engagements were subsidiary to the main action, one of them a salutary reminder that foreknowledge merely gives advantage, it does not guarantee victory. *Münsterland*'s blockade running days were over and it was decided that she should return to German waters, probably for employment in the Baltic trade. In the afternoon of 22 October 1943, British Intelligence learned that she was leaving Brest for Cherbourg.

That evening the cruiser *Charybdis*, two fleet destroyers (speed 32 knots) and four 25-knot Hunts, sailed from Plymouth to intercept. Although such 'Tunnel' sweeps had been taking place for a couple of months, this particular group of ships had never operated or trained together as a unit. Reaching the French coast, the cruiser led the line westwards at 13 knots. This was standard procedure. The Germans' standard procedure was to order coastal convoys into a convenient harbour as soon as their radar screens showed the familiar line of echoes. This night they had prepared something special—a seaward screen of five Elbing torpedo boats. In the ensuing confusion *Charybdis* was torpedoed and sunk, while *Limbourne* had her bows blown off and had to be despatched later. Five hundred men were lost. The lessons of this night led to the formation of the 10th Destroyer Flotilla, a homogeneous force of powerful destroyers which worked together as a team for the whole of 1944. An air raid subsequently damaged *Münsterland* at Cherbourg and she eventually ran aground off Cap Blanc Nez, being finished off by the long-range guns at Dover.

On the other side of the world, it was the Axis who were being ambushed. By now, British and Dutch submarines had been stationed in the Malacca Strait between Sumatra and Malaya to interfere with Japanese coastal traffic and watch out for movements connected with the U-boat base on Penang Island. On 13 November 1943, *Taurus* sighted a large Japanese submarine. The 2198-ton *I34* had set out from Singapore the previous day on a transport mission to Europe. Her voyage was ended by *Taurus*'s torpedoes.

A fortnight later (on 27 November) *U178* departed Penang, as the base was not yet sufficiently developed to undertake the refit of this Type IXD2. Kapitän-leutnant Spahr loaded torpedoes to complete an Indian Ocean war patrol before making for France. A similar programme was planned for Chu-sa Kinashi when he left Penang in *I29* on 16 December 1943. Meanwhile, the first boats of the second Gruppe *Monsun* were getting under way. Those which proceeded into the Atlantic before the end of 1943 were the Type IXD2 *U848*, *U849*, *U850*, and *U177*, plus the Type XB *U219* and a Type IXC—*U510*. Only the last arrived at Penang. *U219* was due to lay mines off Cape Town and Colombo, but was recalled for service as a submarine tanker. Air patrols from Ascension and US escort carriers accounted for the rest.

There was also the possibility that a surface blockade runner might be able to break out in the North Atlantic winter. The Allies learned that such a vessel had been moved from Bordeaux to Concarneau in Brittany, probably to complete the embarkation of U-boat equipment. The German authorities may have believed that she was less likely to be bombed at anchor there, than berthed in Lorient or Brest. An air attack on 1 December 1943 was not successful, but it was repeated on the 18th of the month. Covered by Hawker Typhoons, Bristol Beaufighters of No. 254 Squadron badly damaged the ship with torpedoes and cannon fire. Salvage attempts failed and she later sank off Lorient. So passed *Pietro Orseolo*, now in German hands and being managed by Hamburg-Amerika.

The preliminaries were over and it was time for the main event to begin. Operation Stonewall was co-ordinated by Admiral Sir Ralph Leatham, C-in-C Plymouth. *Gambia* and *Glasgow* sailed on 12 December to patrol an area 500 miles north-northwest of the Azores. One cruiser would be on duty, while the other moored stern-first to a jetty at Horta, fuelling from an oiler stationed there. There was no blackout and there was plenty of food, especially fresh fruit, but it was a difficult harbour to get in and out of. C-in-C Plymouth also co-ordinated air searches, but these were still bedevilled by problems of identification, especially at night. At 0244 on 18 December, a Halifax sighted a 6000-ton merchantman in position 49° 13′ North/09° 25′ West. Subsequent reports estimated her size as 8000 tons and gave a variety of positions. She also opened fire when attacked and special air and sea searches had to be mounted to locate this elusive and hostile vessel. She was eventually identified as the British *LCT573*, displacing a mere 200 tons. Meanwhile these same searches had also reported other contacts, and these too had to be investigated. They proved to be the 270-ton tug *Empire John* (in company with *LCT573*, but not noticed before) and the 1300-ton Indian escort sloop *Godavari* (out looking for the ship first sighted).

When the blockade runner *Osorno* (whose German codename was *Bernau*) was sighted by Coastal Command on Christmas Day, her destruction took precedence over all other targets. Two of the Halifax strike force sighted U-boats during their approach, but ignored them. However, the German escort force put up so much flak and was covered by Ju88 fighters so that *Osorno* was able to reach the Gironde, although she had to be beached there after running onto a wreck.

Kapitän zur See Erdmenger's destroyers had been further reinforced for *Bernau* by the 4th Torpedo Boat Flotilla under Korvettenkapitän Kohlauf, whose *T27*, *T22*, *T23*, *T24*, *T25* and *T26* had taken part in a number of successful Channel engagements. The larger Narvik *Z23* had shipped 200 tons of water and had to make for the shelter of the Spanish coast during part of the *Osorno* operation, but she was able to participate in Operation *Trave* which was the codename assigned to *Alsterufer*; *ZH1* was left behind for this sortie as she had developed condenser trouble. On the morning of 28 December the German destroyers and torpedo boats were still at sea, apparently ignorant of *Alsterufer*'s destruction by Coastal Command. Their movements had been observed by aircraft and Admiral Leatham had diverted the cruisers *Penelope* and *Mauritius* and the minelayer *Ariadne* to cover the area between the Azores and the Iberian peninsula. *Gambia* would sail from Horta to join *Glasgow* and *Enterprise*, the latter fuelling and departing from Plymouth on 27 December.

By the morning of 28 December *Glasgow* and *Enterprise* had rendezvoused and were patrolling much nearer to the French coast than on previous occasions. The First Sea Lord, Admiral of the Fleet Sir Andrew Cunningham, had decided that the risks from German air attacks must be accepted and ordered that they could go as close as 200 miles to the shores of France if that resulted in the successful interception of blockade runners or their destroyer escort.

At 1342, *Glasgow* heading northwest sighted the German destroyers eight miles away to port, steering approximately southeast. The two cruisers immediately hoisted battle ensigns and turned parallel with their opponents, keeping between them and their French base. Fire was opened four minutes later.

The Germans laid a smokescreen through which they occasionally and briefly emerged, straddling *Glasgow* and *Enterprise*, but themselves suffering nearmisses and hits. The German torpedoes were avoided, but one 15-cm (5.9-inch) shell landed on *Glasgow*'s forward boiler room intake, jagged splinters killing two of the crew of the port pompom and wounding six others. It also started a fire in the ready-use magazine. While this was being extinguished the Luftwaffe joined in, but *Glasgow*'s 4-inch (10.2-cm) AA guns forced the Fw200c to turn away. Captain Clark momentarily increased speed so that the radio-controlled glider-bomb it was trying to direct, exploded just astern. Fortunately the two cruisers were not steaming in line ahead.

It will never be known just what Kapitän zur See Erdmenger hoped to do when *Z27* led three ships round to the northwest, while the others headed southwards behind a smokescreen at 1428. Was he sacrificing some of his vessels while the others made their escape, or was he intending to trap the British ships between his two forces? The result of his action was that the two cruisers could now concentrate their fire, pursuing the smaller group westwards. *Glasgow* and *Enterprise* were steadier gun platforms in these heavy seas, while their opponents found that the Narviks' forward mountings could not be worked as well as had been hoped. Just over an hour later, and in spite of another glider-bomb directed at *Enterprise*, *Z27*, *T25* and *T26* had been sunk.

The other destroyers and torpedo boats took no further part in the battle, but they were not allowed to proceed unmolested, being bombed and strafed by British Halifaxes and American PB4Ys (from Bombron 105). Two PB4Ys were lost, but another shot down a Fw200c. Eventually all the surviving German ships made port, *Z32* and *Z37* the Gironde, *Z23* and *T22* St Jean de Luz, and *Z24*, *T23*, *T24* and *T27* Brest.

Glasgow and *Enterprise* returned to Plymouth, to be greeted by congratulations and awards. En route they were subjected to further air attacks, but the ships' own AA barrage and RAF fighters protected them from damage. *Glasgow*'s two dead ratings were buried at sea, their wreath being made from a Christmas tree prepared for a party in the Azores.

Osorno and *Alsterufer* may have passed through the 1700-mile gap between Africa and South America. Vice-Admiral Ingram's forces were determined that no more blockade runners should escape them. Bombron 107 had eleven Consolidated PB4Y-1 Liberators and fifteen crews available, split between Ascension Island and Natal in Brazil. The crews did not have their own personal aircraft; the next team on the roster took off in the next serviceable PB4Y. Their sole function was the interception of the three runners known to be attempting the passage; everything else was of secondary importance.

Each plane flew a triangular search pattern; perhaps 700 miles out, then a 400-mile leg, and another 1000 miles back. According to reference books, the normal range of these machines was 2100 miles, with a theoretical maximum of 2290 miles. There was not much in reserve for full-power combat far from base or for inaccurate navigation on the homeward run. A formation of Army North American B-25 Mitchells, twin-engined bombers with a range of 1275 miles, covered the area immediately around Ascension. The principal warships on duty were those cruisers and destroyers which had been patrolling these waters since before the war began. Their zeal was undiminished and, in the cruiser *Omaha*, was boosted by Captain Leffler's promise of 25 dollars and thirty days' leave to the first lookout who reported a proven blockade runner.

Wideawake Field on Ascension Island was situated on the breeding ground of thousands of sooty terns. The first event of New Year's Day 1944 was the departure of a PB4Y to investigate a suspicious ship sighted far to the north the previous evening by an RAF aircraft from Freetown. Lieutenant Krug had seven and a half hours of seeing nothing but sea ahead of him. The earliest routine patrols lined up on the runway twenty minutes later at 0740. As *Baker 5* lifted off, Lieutenant M.G. Taylor opened up the 4800 hp of four Pratt & Whitney radials; *Baker 9* started rolling. The vibration ceased, the co-pilot swept up the undercarriage lever, the nose and mainwheels disappeared, and the island fell away. The engineer, navigator, bombardier and radioman busied themselves with their respective tasks. Whenever they glanced out of the windows, like the two pilots and the machine-gunners. all they saw was sea and sky, waves and clouds. Somebody produced coffee and a snack meal; they chatted; the aircraft droned on.

At about 1400 they saw something, a ship, a merchant ship heading east-northeast at 10 knots. The radioman sent out the position (09° 35′ North/23° 45′ West) as the PB4Y dropped down to investigate. Fourteen minutes later, and 200 miles away, *Baker 5* was making a similar signal from 07° 52′ South/21° 40′ West. A merchant vessel was claiming to be the British *Seapool*, but did not look exactly like her.

Meanwhile, Lieutenant Taylor was circling the ship which his *Baker 9* had found. She had an upright look to her, straight stem, mast, separate bridge, funnel, mast, kingpost and counter stern. A large British flag was painted on the deck. The Americans consulted the *Manual of Merchant Ships*. Aircraft Ordnanceman 2nd Class Robert E. MacGregor got his camera ready to take a photograph for comparative study back at base. The PB4Y flashed a challenge. Four flags fluttered up a hoist, but were hauled up down again almost at once.

Lieutenant Taylor was now close enough to read a small nameboard on the side of the bridge. *Glenbank*, it said. The British freighter had left Cape Town on 24 December 1943. It could be her. She ought to hoist her secret call sign, but then, Allied merchantmen had become reluctant to answer challenges from four-engined aircraft which in this area were so obviously American. It was early afternoon, the hottest part of the day. Perhaps the crew were suffering from what one official report described as 'normal inactivity' (AI6-3/FVB-107: *Interception and Trailing of the German SS Wesserland*). If so, it was time to wake them up. One of *Baker 9*'s gunners loosed a few .50-inch (12.7-mm) rounds across the stranger's bows.

The effect was instantaneous. The ship opened up with continuous bursts from 3.7-cm (1.5-inch) AA guns, raking the full length of the PB4Y. One shell exploded right on No. 2 Propeller, metal splinters piercing an oil pressure line, an ignition lead and other equipment inside the nacelle. Another round penetrated the port side of the aircraft, shot across the fuselage and into the breech of the starboard waist gun, where it detonated, damaged the VHF radio set. A third projectile exploded on the tunnel hatch, affecting the tail controls and injuring AOM2 MacGregor in the left leg and arm and his right hand. With the wind blowing through the holed fuselage, Lieutenant Taylor feathered the Port Inner, reported the situation by radio, and then set course for base, landing safely at 1845.

The South Atlantic forces now had two suspicious merchantmen to check out. *Baker 9*'s contact could not be *Glenbank*. German agents may have reported reliably that this vessel had indeed left Cape Town, but the real *Glenbank* was bound for Montevideo, and could not be 540 miles west-southwest of Ascension. In any case, she had proved her hostility by opening fire. The destroyer *Somers* (codenamed *Scorpion*) was sent to investigate more closely, while the cruiser *Marblehead* (referred to as *Cutlass*) and the destroyer *Winslow* sought out *Baker 5*'s contact. All through the afternoon, evening and night, on an airfield the Army considered too hazardous for nocturnal operations, Navy planes landed, were fuelled, serviced and took off again with fresh crews. Temporary communications difficulties between warships and aircraft were sorted out.

At 2035, Lieutenant Ford in *Baker 12* found a ship 70 miles to the southeast of the last known position of *Baker 9*'s assailant. Could it be the same ship? If she were a German blockade runner, why was she not farther north of her previous location? Perhaps her master was trying to fool the searchers by doubling back.

By 2200, *Marblehead* and *Winslow* had intercepted *Baker 5*'s suspect. A boarding party had to be sent before she could be positively identified as the British *Seapool*—she just looked different from the air, that was all.

The other ship had still not been verified. Progressive aircraft reports that night and early morning, plotted her track as a series of giant zigzags.

At 0930 on 2 January, exactly six hours after touchdown, *Baker 12* (*USN32065*) was taking the air again. This time she was piloted by Lieutenant R.T. Johnson and his crew, now rested after flying in from Natal in another machine. They were undertaking a normal blockade runner patrol, but soon orders came to abandon all routine missions and concentrate on finding and fixing the alleged

Glenbank. She was to be given one more chance to authenticate herself and then she could be bombed.

Again the situation was confused by two more suspicious but British merchantmen, *Fort Wellington* and *Wascana Park.* The latter had to be boarded by *Somers,* but at 1622, even while Commander W.C. Hughes was closing this vessel, Lieutenant Johnson was investigating an object 60 miles away. He took *Baker 12* round in a circle, transmitting automatic MOs (or homing signals) to guide in other PB4Ys and *Somers.* The identity of the ship had still not been proved, but at 1725 she showed she was not of Allied nationality by opening fire when *Baker 12* came in too close. There was one hit, causing a minor fuel leak in the wing tanks. There was no damage to the radio equipment, and the homing signals still went out good and strong. Lieutenant Johnson continued to circle, until by 1830 there were three aircraft orbiting the target. Now, at last, Lieutenant Johnson decided he could leave and *Baker 12* set course for Ascension over 600 miles away. But every twenty seconds, another gallon of gasoline streamed into the darkening atmosphere. *Baker 2* kept company but the messages from Lieutenant Johnson told their own story.

2128: 'Ditching SOS—60 to 90 miles. Sending MO's (8340).'
2130: 'Going down—dropping flares.'
   'Two engines out. Altitude 1400 feet.'
   'Number 4 engine oil pressure fluctuating.'
   'Both engines oil pressure fluctuating.'
   'Number 3 engine oil pressure quivering. Don't look like it will hold up. Altitude 600 feet.'
2141: 'Sending MO's (8340).'
2145: 'One engine OK—other doubtful [garbled] 600 feet [garbled].'
2147: Signal stopped.

US Navy PB4Y *No. 32605* went down under the Southern Cross with all hands.

Her sister-plane circled until she too ran low on fuel and had to head for home. But Lieutenant Johnson had achieved his mission. At 2200 *Somers'* crew saw flares being dropped from an aircraft 12 miles away. Beneath that illumination was a zigzagging ship. An hour later she had been given enough chances and Commander Hughes ordered his 5-inch (12.7-cm) guns to fire at a range of four miles. There was no return fire and the target was soon being hit hard. Five men were killed and she went down half an hour after midnight. At 0400 on 3 January *Somers* made another signal, 'SHIP NOW SUNK. IDENTIFIED AS WESSERLAND. 134 SURVIVORS IN GERMAN NAVAL UNIFORM' (A16-3/FVB-107: *Interception and Trailing of the German SS Wesserland*). *Omaha*'s War Diary commented: 'It's our turn next' (NRS 1977/106: *USS Omaha War Diary*).

At 0955 on 4 January, *Omaha* and *Jouett* were some 550 miles northeast of Brazil, when Seaman First Class P.J. Kraynik earned himself that reward for spotting another blockade runner 16 miles away. While one scoutplane maintained anti-submarine watch, the other circled the stranger which made an American call-sign. *Rio Grande*'s First Officer wanted to open fire, but Kapitän von Allwörden said that there was no point. As the two warships closed in, there was an explosion right aft and smoke began to pour from *Rio Grande*. *Omaha* and *Jouett* opened fire, green and red dyes distinguishing their shell splashes. The destroyer also used automatic fire to try to force the crew back aboard, but the rest of the scuttling charges went off. *Rio Grande* sank at 1056 to Kapitän von Allwörden's salute and three cheers for a gallant ship, called for by Kapitän Bansen, one of the passengers. The lifeboats, whose occupants included a pet wolfhound, made for the Brazilian coast, but were located by a blimp and picked up by *Marblehead*.

Next day, while *Jouett* was recovering samples of rubber and lard from the surrounding sea, a Martin PBM Mariner from Patron (Patrol Squadron) 203 at Natal, was challenging a merchant ship called *Floridian* some 50 miles to the south. There was no such vessel on the pilot's location plot and her description fitted that of *Burgenland*. Before another PBM could arrive, *Omaha* and *Jouett* were on the scene, their crews going to action stations without waiting for General Quarters to be sounded. Radar contact and visual sighting was followed by challenge. *Omaha* also fired two shots across her bow, and then both warships opened fire as the scuttling charges detonated. Soon *Burgenland* was ablaze and settling by the stern, going down at 1758. The crew had been ready to abandon ship and all 150 were rescued—with one exception. The American warships, assisted by the minelaying corvette *Camocim* and the tug *Poti* (both Brazilian) also recovered 2000 bales of rubber from the sea, enough for 5000 aircraft tyres. Thus German effort aided the Allies' war industry. Of the five cargoes despatched from the Far East, only 6890 tons had reached France—and that had had to be salvaged from *Osorno*.

There remained the question of what had happened to the five criminals sent to Germany during this series of voyages. The three imprisoned in *Osorno* came ashore to whatever harsh punishment awaited them. One, alleged to have been a Soviet agent, was shot by his guard just before *Burgenland* was abandoned. The other, accused of a much less serious offence, went down in *Rio Grande*. Later that month, SKL approved the order that had led to their deaths, as a warning to all traitors.

17 *Monsun*

It now seemed that all surface blockade running was out of the question. Only one out of five merchantmen despatched from Japan in the winter of 1943–4 had reached Europe—and she had run aground. Even so, the tonnage which *Osorno* had delivered was far in excess of anything that submarines could carry until the completion of the Type XX boats in the summer of 1945. Therefore, argued Grossadmiral Dönitz at the Führer's Naval Conference of 18 January 1944, Germany's mercantile marine must try again. Eight ships were available in Bordeaux, four of them loaded ready to sail. If only one of them successfully completed a round trip, it would be worth the risk. The German war effort needed that rubber and wolfram from the Far East.

Not so, replied Hitler. German wolfram requirements could be maintained by a regular number of small shipments from the Iberian peninsula. Why not assign all possible vessels to that trade before it was cut off by Allied pressure? Secondly, he did not believe that those four blockade runners would ever reach Japan, let alone get back again. Finally, he did not believe that the supply of natural rubber was as vital as Dönitz claimed. He had figures to prove it. Tyres made from artificial rubber would last nearly 25,000 miles at a speed of 40–45 mph. Natural rubber was good for only half that distance. Where he had got these figures from was immaterial. Whether they referred to a constant-speed laboratory experiment, or to damaged wheels bouncing through the debris of shattered streets and then racing along the autobahn, did not matter. Der Führer had spoken.

Grossadmiral Dönitz had too many other things to do and was too much of a realist to debate a losing proposition. Outward-bound voyages were cancelled, while arrangements made for those vessels still in the Far East to be utilized as supply ships or transferred to Japanese service. Those overseas products which, in spite of der Führer's opinion, were still demanded by German industry, would have to travel some other way. Was there any alternative to the employment of U-boats in this traffic? Hardly. Even the smuggling of very small items such as documents, drugs, diamonds and platinum, was being intercepted.

Neutral ships were still liable to interception and search by Contraband Control. From 1943 onwards the Gibraltar Examination Centre was probably the most important, ensuring that nothing found its way to Germany via Spain and Portugal. Officers encountered the same protests about bringing ships and passengers into hazardous areas as early in the war, but they also became expert in locating hidden compartments in crew furniture, passengers' luggage and cargo containers. At this level it was called smuggling rather than blockade running, but the individuals participating did not always do so for personal gain alone. There were patriotic agents and idealists as well as those who saw an opportunity to make money. Such activities were not encouraged by neutral masters and shipowners; they had no wish to be blacklisted with all sorts of postwar consequences.

There was nothing for it, but to use submarines as blockade runners. In any case, Gruppe *Monsun*, both war and support boats, might as well come back with useful cargoes at the end of their Indian Ocean duty. So, the U-boats departed, doing 12 knots on the surface whenever they could, but usually creeping along submerged at a mere 4 knots, unable to charge the failing batteries or ventilate the foetid, fearful atmosphere. By day or night, the radar-seeing aircraft found them. Already the alarm was sounding. Lookouts and captain tumbled down the ladder, locked the hatch, and the U-boat headed for 'the cellar'. Sometimes the warning came too late, cannon-shells piercing the hull, depth-charges lifting the boat, fracturing pipes and engine-seatings, electricity racing across the motor room, one and a half tons of torpedo coming adrift. Sometimes the boat continued its fatal sliding dive. Sometimes there was a brief hiatus on the surface, a Niagara-filled hatchway being the only exit. Sometimes the boat escaped with a shaking. Sometimes nothing happened; the airmen had not seen the diving boat, or the aircraft was only a distant seagull. The sky was always their enemy.

Monsun commanders were ordered not to attract attention while on passage, but all along their route they were hunted by RAF Coastal Command, American escort carriers, US Navy PB4Ys, South African bombers and Royal Navy carrier aircraft. Even nearing their goal, the crews could not relax. The island-filled straits of the Indies concealed mines parachuted from long-range bombers or deposited by Allied submarines which also lay in wait outside U-boat bases. Those boats which survived this ordeal and the growing strength of Allied anti-submarine forces in the Indian Ocean then had to run the same gauntlet to reach home. A list of departures and arrivals tells its own story:-

3 January 1944: *U1062* (Type VIIF) departed Bergen with a cargo of thirty-nine torpedoes for Gruppe *Monsun*. The group was so short of torpedoes that

three shorter-ranged Type IXC40 boats at Penang, were ordered to embark strategic materials and come home via their patrol areas in the Indian Ocean.

4 January: *U532* departed Penang in accordance with the previous instructions.

9 January: *U188* departed Penang under similar orders as *U532*.

18 January: *U852* (Type IXD2) departed Kiel. En route Kapitänleutnant Eck sank the freighter *Peleus* in the Atlantic, but tried to keep his presence secret by eliminating all floating evidence of his attack. Later, *U852* was driven ashore in the Indian Ocean by RAF Wellingtons. After the war, Kapitän-leutnant Eck was tried and sentenced to death for killing the *Peleus* survivors.

26 January: *UIT22* (ex-Italian *Bagnolini*) departed Bordeaux with Monsun stores.

28 January: *U168* departed Penang for a war patrol in the Indian Ocean before proceeding to Europe.

February: *U843*, *U801* (both Type IXC) and *U851* (Type IXD2) departed France. *U801* was sunk by US carrier aircraft, a destroyer and a destroyer escort in the Atlantic. *U851* simply disappeared.

9 February: *UIT24* (ex-Italian *Comandante Cappellini*) departed Penang with cargo for Bordeaux.

10 February: *U183* departed Penang as per the orders to *U532*.

All these boats proceeding in both directions were to fuel from oilers stationed in the Indian Ocean, *Charlotte Schliemann* being on duty at present. Such rendezvous could not be set up without appropriate signal traffic to and from interested U-boats. This was intercepted and deciphered by Allied intelligence. The tanker was actually fuelling *U532* 950 miles east of Madagascar when a Mauritius-based Catalina came in sight on 11 February. The destroyer *Relentless*, 100 miles away, covered the distance at full speed, her 4.7-inch (11.9-cm) shells and a torpedo hurrying the tanker's scuttling procedure. Forty-one prisoners were taken up and later more survivors were rescued when *U532* surfaced. The boat spent three days evading depth-charge attacks. Until the oiler *Brake* arrived on station, those U-boats at sea in the Indian Ocean kept going by sharing each other's bunkers.

15 February: *UIT23* (formerly the Italian *Reginaldo Giuliani*), called at Penang, three days after leaving Singapore with a cargo for Europe. She was torpedoed by a British submarine, appropriately named *Tally-Ho*.

March: *U1059* (Type VIIF) departed Europe with a cargo of *Monsun* torpedoes. She was sunk by US escort carrier aircraft in the Atlantic. The Type IXD2 *U181*, *U196* and *U198* plus *U537* (Type IXC40) departed Europe. *U198* was sunk by anti-submarine vessels with aircraft assistance in the Indian Ocean.

11 March: Operation Kiefer (Pinetree); the Japanese *I29* met the Type IXC *U518* in outer Biscay. Both boats were escorted into Bordeaux by *Z23*, *ZH1*, *T27* and *T29*. This was the last time German surface warships ventured into the broad Atlantic.

Meanwhile *U178* had been ordered to fuel the eastbound transport *UIT22*, whose diesel tanks had been damaged by air attack off Ascension. Allied direction finders and decoders learned that the rendezvous was off the Cape of Good Hope. *U178* was attacked first, but Kapitänleutnant Wilhelm Spahr was a veteran submariner—he had been the Navigating Officer when *U47* had sunk the battleship *Royal Oak* in Scapa Flow in 1939. *U178* survived Ventura bombing on 8 March, evading Ventura and Catalina patrols by staying down during the hours of daylight.

On the morning of 11 March, a Catalina from No. 262 RAF Squadron sighted a U-boat, but not the one they had been hunting earlier. This was *UIT22*, and her commander elected to stay on the surface and fight back with automatic weapons. Some damage was inflicted on the Catalina, but *UIT22* had been fatally depth-charged. Diving, she was strafed and depth-charged by two more flying boats whenever she tried to surface. When Kapitänleutnant Spahr arrived at the rendezvous fifteen hours later, there was only oil to greet him, and *U178* submerged for the rest of the day.

Other intelligence reports suggested more blockade runners or supply vessels in the Indian Ocean. Two task forces totalling two aircraft carriers, four cruisers and four destroyers were formed to search them out. On 12 March, one of *Battler*'s Swordfish caught sight of *Brake* while fuelling two U-boats 1500 miles southeast of Madagascar. The biplane summoned *Roebuck* to the scene. *Brake*'s scuttling charges went off and the wreck was shelled for an hour. Later *U168* and *U188* rescued the survivors. *U532* had completed oiling earlier, and *U188* almost so, but the fuel situation for the other Indian Ocean U-boats was desperate. Again, by pooling their resources, they all managed to reach port, though not necessarily their intended ones. *U532*, *UIT24* and *U183* all returned to Penang, while *U168* went to Djakarta. Only *U188* was able to round the Cape of Good Hope and make for France.

16 April: *I29* departed Bordeaux.

19 April: *U1062* arrived Penang.

April: *U859* and *U860* (both Type IXD2) sailed from Kiel, the latter being sunk by US escort carrier aircraft in the South Atlantic. *U1224*, a Type IXC, was handed over to her Japanese crew, renumbered *Ro501* and left Norway for Japan. A US destroyer escort sank her in the Atlantic.

23 April: the newly commissioned *I52* left Singapore on the first stage of Operation Tanne-Föhre (Fir-Tree), another transport exchange. Allied intelligence monitored her Atlantic rendezvous with *U530*. On 23 June 1944, the Japanese boat received radar warning equipment, but a new device was now entering the Allied armoury. Automatic sonobuoys were being dropped

to broadcast sonar echoes to aircraft circling overhead. Two US carrier-borne Avengers thus kept in touch with *I52* and sank her that same night.

6 May: *U490*, a Type XIV tanker, departed Kristiansund to make up for the loss of supply ships in the Indian Ocean. Her Atlantic fate was sealed by another of the American escort carrier groups.

25 May: *U178* arrived Bordeaux, bales of rubber helping to keep her rickety engines in place.

19 June: *U188* arrived Bordeaux.

June: *U861* and *U862* (both Type IXD2) left Norwegian waters. *U843* arrived Penang after being damaged by aircraft in the Atlantic.

6 July: *U1062*, the VIIF transport, set out on her return voyage from Penang· She was intercepted by an escort carrier group in the central Atlantic on 5 October 1944. *USS Fessenden* completed her destruction with depth-charges.

26 July: *U863* (Type IXD2) departed Trondheim. She was sunk near Ascension by two PB4Ys of Bombron 107. On this day *I29* was proceeding north of the Philippines on the last lap of her transport journey from Bordeaux via Penang and Singapore. The area was patrolled by the US submarine *Sawfish*. *I29* was torpedoed and sunk.

2 August: *U537* arrived Djakarta.

August: *U196* arrived Penang.

20 August: *U180* and *U195* were the two Type IXD1 boats whose high-speed diesels emitted clouds of smoke. They had now been completely converted to the transport role by the Bordeaux yard. More reliable diesels had been installed and both vessels sailed as part of the general evacuation from French ports following the Allied landings. Together with *U219*, a Type XB mine-layer also adapted as a transport, they were bound for the Far East. Their journey down the river was lengthy because of Allied control of the air. *U180* had got only as far as the Gironde estuary when she detonated a mine and sank on 22 August.

31 August: *U871* (Type IXD2) departed Trondheim. An RAF Flying Fortress from the Azores ended her career.

23 September: *U859* survived the Atlantic passage and an Indian Ocean war patrol. Arriving off Penang, she was torpedoed by the British submarine *Trenchant*.

The Straits of Malacca had become a death-trap, the Indian Ocean as danger-ous as the Atlantic. Penang had never been an effective base. The place was unhealthy; it lacked European food and skilled dockyard labout; it lacked stockpiles of spare parts, ammunition and torpedoes. It could take up to two months for a normal refit between patrols. It lacked the enthusiastic co-operation of a cheerful ally; the Japanese had never been over-friendly, and they were becoming decidedly hostile now that the war was going badly. Supply ships could no longer operate in the Indian Ocean, so that U-boats would have to spend too much time on passage to and from well-defended target areas.

The order went out to Fregattenkapitän Dommes to leave Penang and go to Djakarta which was nearer the Indonesian oilfields and afforded immediate access to the expanses of the Indian Ocean through the Sunda Strait. He had to get his boats ready for sea, load as much cargo as possible, plus any serviceable torpedoes, and send them home. By now, French ports were out of the question. Those which had not been overrun were themselves having to be supplied by submarine. The *Monsun* U-boats would have to go northabout, making for Norwegian waters via the Greenland Strait or through the Iceland-Faeroes gap. Because none of them were fitted with snorkel, they would have to surface in order to recharge their batteries. That meant passing through the most dangerous zone during the dark storms of the North Atlantic winter. The blockade runners' war was ending the way it had begun.

Each boat sailed as soon as she was ready. The roll of disasters continued:

4 October: *U168* departed Djakarta. She proceeded along the north coast of Java on the surface, her diesels smoking badly because of the poor-quality fuel. At 0641 on 6 October 1944, she was sighted by Lieutenant-Commander H.A.W. Goossens in *Zwaardvisch*, a British T-class submarine now serving in the Royal Netherlands Navy. Six torpedoes were fired at five-second intervals from a distance of 900 yards. The first missed ahead, the second exploded in *U168*'s bows, and the third and fourth hit the control and engine rooms, but failed to detonate. Those not killed by the explosion went down with the boat to a depth of 120 feet. Lieutenant-Commander Goossens surfaced to take six survivors on board, but soon found another twenty-one bobbing up around him—most without an escape lung. He picked them all up and, apart from Kapitänleutnant Pich, three officers and a wounded rating, transferred the rest to a distant fishing boat.

19 October: *U181* departed Djakarta. She got almost as far as South Africa, sinking an American freighter en route, but her propeller shaft was giving trouble. She had to turn back to Djakarta, arriving there on 5 January 1945.

8 November: *U537* departed Djakarta, heading east along the Javanese coast so that she could pass through one of the channels through the Lesser Sunda Islands; perhaps it would not be watched so closely as the main exit past Krakatoa. *U537* made good speed and next day was already approaching Balinese waters, guarded by the US submarine *Flounder*. No U-boat could survive the detonation of four torpedoes.

11 November: *U196* departed Djakarta via the Sunda Strait. That was the last

ever heard of her. It was later learned that the British submarine *Porpoise* had laid a minefield in the area. *U510* also set out, but returned with engine trouble.

10 December: *U843* departed Djakarta, fuelling en route from the eastbound U195, which arrived in the Far East with U219.

6 January: *U510* departed Penang.

13 January: *U532* departed Penang.

14 January: *U861* departed Djakarta.

17 January: *U195* departed Djakarta. Her engines were not up to the strain of another long voyage. She topped up *U532*'s tanks and returned to Djakarta on 3 March 1945.

5 February: *U864* (Type IXD2) departed Bergen for the Far East. Four days later she was torpedoed and sunk by the British submarine *Venturer*.

During February 1945, the South African forces learned that a U-boat was trying to slip past their patrols, but Fregattenkapitän Junker was skilful and evaded the searchers. On the 23rd he coolly surfaced to finish off the torpedoed freighter *Point Pleasant Park* with gunfire. Two more merchantmen were sunk by *U532* during her northward passage in March 1945. She kept well to the west, sliding past the American coast before steering across the Atlantic.

Meanwhile the Germans were making one final effort to help their Axis partners during the last days of the war in Europe. On 1 April 1945, the Type XB *U234* set out to return two Japanese aviation and submarine experts to their homeland. Chu-sa Tomonaga and Chu-sa Soji took with them sample pieces of equipment. Next day, *U843* arrived in Bergen, but her cargo never arrived in Germany. Crossing the Kattegat, she was sunk by RAF Mosquitoes. She was followed by *U861* on 18 April, but this boat remained in Norwegian waters with 144 tons of wolfram, iodine, tin and rubber. *U510* ran so low on fuel that she had to put into St Nazaire and surrender to the Allied forces. Out in the Far East, on 24 April, *U183* was hurrying through the Java Sea, having left Djakarta two days previously. The large Rising Sun she wore proclaimed her friendship to Japanese observers and her hostility to the American submarine *Besugo*. There was one survivor from *U183*.

On VE-Day, all the German U-boats and merchantmen still scattered through the Far East were taken over by the Japanese. The Japanese officers in *U234* committed suicide, rather than accompany the Germans as they set course to surrender their boat at Portsmouth, New Hampshire. Two Type IXD2 boats (*U874* and *U875*) were loading with a combined total of 170 tons of mercury, lead and optical glass, but they never left European waters.

And then there was one—one homeward-bound blockade runner, loaded with raw materials. On VE-Day she was off the Faeroes. Fregattenkapitän Junker surfaced, displaying the black flag of surrender. In Liverpool Docks, which had seen the Atlantic convoys of two world wars and the blockade runners of the American Civil War, *U532* discharged her cargo. There were 110 tons of tin ingots, 8 tons of wolfram, 4 tons of molybdenum, and smaller amounts of selenium, quinine and crystals. There were also tube-like containers holding 8 tons of rubber—rubber for the tyres of agricultural tractors, delivery lorries and private cars—raw materials for the reconstruction of Europe in the days of peace.

18 Where Lies the Land?

From 1941 to 1944, Axis ships trading directly between the Far East and Occupied Europe delivered 43,891 tons of natural rubber for use by German and Italian industry. Edible oils, wolfram, tin, opium, quinine and other Oriental products made up another 68,117 tons. Over a hundred other vessels, including prizes, had reached German-held destinations from trans-ocean ports in 1939–42. Not all of them were fully laden, but their cargoes included a variety of foodstuffs, fuels, raw materials and manufactured goods at a time when everything had its use in the war effort. In the reverse direction, 56,987 tons of machinery, finished items, chemicals, documents and technical samples arrived in Japan. Japanese scientists and industrialists tried to incorporate the German research in their own projects. They were hindered and finally prevented by the severance of Japan's ocean trade-routes and by the aerial devastation of the home islands. At the other end of the partnership, German industry benefitted much more from the tonnage which arrived by sea, yet that amount was small compared with the total consumption of artificial and European products. Was it worth the nineteen merchantmen and sixteen warships lost in the rubber traffic alone, quite apart from all those other merchantmen scuttled or captured in forlorn attempts to break the British blockade in 1939–42?

However, the war economy of Nazi-dominated Europe was nearly self-sufficient, much more so than Britain or Japan. Those overseas products which did get through at such cost in lives and effort were the very items which German scientists could not create artificially, at least not in significant quantities or at the same standard as the natural original. Perhaps it was in their absence that the true worth of these commodities became apparent. Without natural rubber, a tyre might burst, turning over a training aircraft and killing a promising night-fighter pilot temporarily assigned to duty as a flying instructor; a staff car might be delayed en route to an important conference; or a draughtsman smudge the notes on a drawing board, so that the next clerk misread the figures and all the calculations had to be done again. Without good quality metals the bearings in a mobile pump might seize up at the scene of a fire. Without proper vitamins, a factory worker might be forced to have the day off with a migraine headache. Without drugs to deaden the pain, the screams of a wounded man might echo through the shocked wards of a military hospital.

Perhaps a measure of the importance of Axis blockade running is gained from the Allied attitude towards it. Once resources were available, no effort was spared in concentrating warships, aircraft and intelligence agencies on the interception of this traffic. Admittedly, the seizure of contraband did not win the war in 1939 as had been confidently hoped; German industry was too well prepared. But by 1942, the strategic Achilles heel of German industry had been identified and, together with the growing aerial bombardment of the factories and cities themselves, was attacked relentlessly. The establishment of efficient forces and their bases in the South, central and North Atlantic, made it impossible for all but the occasional blockade runner to approach Europe without being sighted somewhere along the route.

In the end, it was the German leadership that lost confidence in the programme and decided the risks were too great, that increasing effort was being expended for diminishing returns. The seamen who crewed freighters and submarines, even those who had lost heart in Axis promises, still took their ships to sea, trusting in skill, bluff and luck. They faced the same hazards as Allied merchant seamen, but without ocean escort. They may have been spared the frustrating tensions of slow convoy, but they knew the loneliness of a completely hostile sea, when any sighting could only be an enemy. Perhaps the nearest equivalent from a British point of view would be trying to imagine merchant ships attempting to take cargoes from Australia to Vladivostock in 1942.

Most international crises since World War II have involved some sort of blockade. So there have been various attempts to evade patrolling warships and aircraft, which have usually claimed international law on their side. Aeroplanes were used to maintain the population and industry of West Berlin during the Russian obstruction of land access in 1948–9. The rapid expansion of the Jewish population was an important stage in the establishment of the state of Israel. Carrying thousands of passengers at a time, old merchantmen, ferry boats and demilitarized warships tried to reach the shore of Palestine, but according to the terms of the British mandate, these people were illegal immigrants. Sighted by aircraft and intercepted by destroyers, the ships were arrested and taken to the port of Haifa or, if still seaworthy, escorted to some more distant harbour. Their passengers were sent to detention camps until Israel gained independence in 1948.

Ships were engaged in gun-running in rebel conflicts in the East Indies, while from 1950 to 1953, United Nations warships imposed a blockade of the Korean coast, although this was more to prevent coastal traffic and fishing than to intercept overseas trade. The same was largely true of the American blockade of

Vietnam from 1964 to 1973. The American cordon around Cuba in 1962 was something different. Destroyers deliberately intercepted 'contraband'-carrying merchantmen on the high seas and turned them back under threat of war. It could not be strictly termed a blockade, since the United States and the Soviet Union were not engaged in hostilities. Nor, according to the old definition, was it a blockade, when the Nigerian government closed its Biafran ports in order to cut off supplies to the insurgents. The sanctions that were imposed after Rhodesia's unilateral declaration of independence were enforced by the Royal Navy intercepting ships suspected of carrying prohibited cargoes to ports in Mozambique for onward shipment by rail.

It seems that modern nations find the weapon of economic blockade, whatever its exact legal terminology, an effective method of enforcing their will upon their opponents. It stops short of outright war. Both sides can compromise via third parties without losing face. If shooting does occur, there is still the possibility of it being confined to two ships on the high seas.

The other side of the story also holds equally true. If blockaded people want something badly enough, there are always enterprising men and women ready to satisfy that demand. They may be inspired by idealism, adventure, duty or money, they may be hailed as heroes, or castigated as mercenary smugglers, but they risk death, liberty and fortune on just one more trip, depending on skill and bluff to see them through—plus luck. Modern methods of communications surveillance, satellite observation and centralized identity checks are so much more sophisticated than the devices which, established on the islands and shores of the Indian and Atlantic Oceans, prevented Axis blockade runners effectively passing between the Far East and Europe. Yet things do not always work perfectly. There are often so many bona fide passengers to be checked, so many genuine craft to be investigated to find the real contraband carrier, that that delay is just long enough for someone else to get through and deliver the goods. It is the luck of the game, a game known to any blockade runner setting out on his lonely journey towards some secret destination in surface ship, submarine, aeroplane or—or space vehicle?

> Where lies the land to which the ship would go?
> Far, far ahead is all her seamen know.
> And where the land she travels from? Away,
> Far, far behind, is all that they can say.
>
>   Arthur Hugh Clough

Bibliography

A16-3/FVB-107: *Interception and Trailing of the German SS Wesserland*, US Navy
  Historical Center
Patrick Abbazia, *Mr Roosevelt's Navy*, USNI, Annapolis, USA, 1975
ADM1/9545: *Contraband Control Service Organisation*, PRO
ADM1/9755: *HMS California Capture of SS Borkum*, PRO
ADM1/10439: *German SS Wahehe*, PRO
ADM1/10593: *Interception of German Merchant Vessels*, PRO
ADM1/10601: *HMS Despatch Report of Proceedings*, PRO
ADM1/10624: *HMS York Report of Proceedings 1-10/3/40*, PRO
ADM1/10645: *Capture of German SS Morea by HMS Hasty on 12/2/40*, PRO
ADM1/10658: *Report of Proceedings from HMS Despatch*, PRO
ADM1/11111: *Economic Warfare Division*, PRO
ADM1/11710: *Identification of Suspicious Merchant Ships*, PRO
ADM1/12030: *Cypher Log of HMS Cheshire*, PRO
ADM1/12033: *Encounter between HMS Durban and Unknown Ship on Friday,
  13 March 1942*, PRO
ADM1/12272: *HMS Dunedin*, PRO
ADM1/12476: *HMS Adventure Interception and Sinking of MV Silvaplana*, PRO
ADM1/12665: *Italian Sloop Eritrea*, PRO
ADM1/12883: *Disguised Enemy Raiders and Blockade Runners*, PRO
ADM1/14426: *US Submarine Shad*, PRO
ADM1/17374: *HNethM Submarine Zwaardvisch*, PRO
ADM1/18914: *Madame Tart*, PRO
ADM1/18939: *Behaviour of British Captured Naval Personnel on board German Ship
  Portland*, PRO
ADM199/390: *Northern Patrol*, PRO
ADM199/549: *German–Japanese Blockade Running*, PRO
ADM199/635: *War Diary West Africa Command 1943*, PRO
ADM199/969: *Reports of Proceedings of HM Ships on South Atlantic Station*, PRO
ADM199/1844: *Tuna Patrol Report*, PRO
ADM199/1861: *HMS Truant Patrol Report*, PRO
Rear-Admiral Paul Auphan & Jacques Mordal, *The French Navy in World War II*,
  USNI, Annapolis, USA, 1959
Jochen Brennecke, *Schwarze Schiffe, Weite See*, Gerhard Stalling, Oldenburg, 1958
Martin H. Brice, *Blockade Runners*, War Monthly, 1976
Chicago Daily News, May 1943
F0371/36002/Z9586: *Attitude of Men of the French Navy, 14 August 1943*, PRO
Aldo Fraccaroli, *Italian Warships of World War II*, Ian Allan, 1968
Lieutenant-Commander G.H. Gill, *Royal Australian Navy 1939–45*,
  Australia in the War of 1939–1945, Australian War Memorial, Canberra, 1957

Geoffrey Jones, *Under Three Flags*, William Kimber, 1973

Arnold Kludas, *Die Schiffe der deutschen Afrika–Linien*, Stalling Oldenburg, 1975

H.T. Lenton, *German Submarines*, Macdonald, 1965

H.T. Lenton & J.J. Colledge, *Warships of World War II*, Ian Allan, 1964

C.E. Lucas-Phillips, *Cockleshell Heroes*, Heinemann, 1956

W.N. Medlicott, *The Economic Blockade*, HMSO, 1952

Theo Michaux, *Rohstoffe aus Ostasien*, Wehrwissenschaftliche Rundschau, 1955/11

Ulrich Mohr & A.V. Sellwood, *Atlantis*, New English Library, 1974

NRS1971/61: *US Atlantic Fleet Cruiser Division 2*, US Naval Historical Center

NRS1977/106: *USS Omaha War Diary*, US Naval Historical Center

Peace between the Allied and Associated Powers and Germany, HMSO, 1919

Kenneth Poolman, *Ark Royal*, New English Library, 1974

Hans Georg Prager, *DDG Hansa*, Koehlers, Herford, 1976

Purnell & Sons, *History of the Second World War*, British Printing Corporation, 1968

Denis Richards & Hilary St George Saunders, *Royal Air Force 1939–1945*, HMSO, 1954

Carlo de Risio et al., *La Marina Italiana Nella Seconda Guerra Mondiale* (especially Vol XVII *I Violatori Di Blocco*), *Ufficio Storico Della Marina Militare*, Roma, 1963

J. Rohwer & G. Hümmelchen, *Chronology of the War at Sea 1939–1945*, Ian Allan, 1972

Captain S.W. Roskill, *The War at Sea 1939–45*, HMSO, 1961

Bernard Stubbs, *The Navy at War*, Faber & Faber, 1940

J.C. Taylor, *German Warships of World War II*, Ian Allan, 1966

L.C.F. Turner, H.R. Gordon-Cumming & J.E. Betzler, *War in the Southern Oceans 1939–45*, Oxford University Press, Cape Town, 1961

Anthony J. Watts, *Japanese Warships of World War II*, Ian Allan, 1966

Hans Jürgen Witthoft, *Die Rohstoff-Blockadebrecher*, publisher unknown

Joachim Wölfer, *Cap Arcona*, Koehlers, Herford, 1977

Index of Ships

General Index